PANZER RECONNAISSANCE

OSPREY
PUBLISHING

PANZER RECC

NNAISSANCE

Thomas Anderson

OSPREY PUBLISHING

Bloomsbury Publishing Plc
Kemp House, Chawley Park, Cumnor Hill, Oxford
OX2 9PH, UK
29 Earlsfort Terrace, Dublin 2, Ireland
1385 Broadway, 5th Floor, New York, NY 10018, USA
E-mail: info@ospreypublishing.com
www.ospreypublishing.com

OSPREY is a trademark of Osprey Publishing Ltd

First published in Great Britain in 2023

ISBN: HB 9781472855022;
eBook 9781472855015;
ePDF 9781472855008;
XML 9781472855039

23 24 25 26. 27   10 9 8 7 6 5 4 3 2 1

Conceived and edited by Jasper Spencer-Smith.
Page Layout: Crispin Goodall.
Index by Michael Napier.
Produced for Bloomsbury Publishing Plc by **Editworks Ltd**.
Printed and bound in India by Replika Press Private Ltd.

Osprey Publishing supports the Woodland Trust, the UK's
leading woodland conservation charity.

To find out more about our authors and books visit
www.ospreypublishing.com. Here you will find extracts,
author interviews, details of forthcoming events and the
option to sign up for our newsletter.

CONTENTS

Introduction

Reconnaissance assets of all kinds have been used throughout the history of conflict to gain advantage over the enemy. Depending on its quality and relevance, this intelligence has been able to contribute decisively to decision-making at the highest echelons of military leadership. The outcomes of many engagements and battles have been significantly influenced by reconnaissance.

Military intelligence generally operates at three levels. Strategic intelligence gathers information on a global scale, using a wide variety of sources and techniques. It primarily serves the decision-making by political leaders. Operational reconnaissance covers the potential or actual battlefield and is conducted at the level of large units such as army groups or armies. It operates deep behind enemy lines. Smaller units engaged in direct combat use all the possibilities of active tactical reconnaissance. Specialized subunits are tasked with gaining knowledge about the condition and navigability of the terrain close to the front, as well as with assessing the strength and operational readiness of the enemy.

After the end of World War I, initial attempts were made in Germany to modernize their reconnaissance forces. Key companies in German industry developed wheeled armoured vehicles that were very advanced for the period, although their performance is often overestimated. After the formation of the *Wehrmacht* (defence force) in 1935, these modern armoured reconnaissance vehicles proved far too complex and expensive for various manufacturers to produce. The situation was exacerbated by shortages material due to a lack of raw materials.

In order to provide the newly created Panzer divisions with suitable reconnaissance elements, simple armoured cars were initially produced and introduced from 1930 onwards, abandoning almost all innovations.

Opposite: In 1936, German reconnaissance troops were initially equipped with basic Adler-built *Kübelwagen* (bucket seat car) which utilized the chassis of a commercial passenger car. Behind the second vehicle is a *leichter Panzerspähwagen* (le PzSpWg – light armoured car) *Sonderkraftfahrzeug* (SdKfz – special purpose vehicle) 221.

Above: Elements of a *Aufklärungs-Kompanie* (AufklKp – reconnaissance company) at their home garrison. In the foreground are three lightly armoured *Kraftfahrzeug* (Kfz – motor vehicle) 13 and a *Kübelwagen* (bucket-seat vehicle); both types were built on the same Adler chassis. Behind them are a number of SdKz 231 (6-Rad) and SdKfz 232 (6-Rad) *schwerer Panzerspähwagen* (s PzSpWg – heavy armoured cars).

Right: The Nazi government made extensive use of lavish parades to demonstrate its military power to the German population and observers from foreign countries.

Initially development was slow. Due to the restrictions imposed under the terms of the Versailles Treaty, resources were limited and secrecy necessary. But this was soon to accelerate significantly in conjunction with the build-up of the German armoured forces. In 1937, a new generation of modern reconnaissance vehicles began to be delivered to units available: the *Vierrad* (4-Rad – four wheel) and *Achtrad* (8-Rad – 8-wheel) *Panzerspähwagen* (PzSpWg – armoured car).

These vehicles provided the basis for the new German reconnaissance detachments of the *motorisiert* (mot – motorized) divisions and the Panzer divisions. During *Unternehmen* (Operation) *Barbarossa* in the Soviet Union this early equipment reached its limits and new solutions were developed and introduced. Now, half-track and tracked vehicles were deployed to fulfill the important task of ground-based reconnaissance even under the most difficult terrain conditions. At the same time, heavy weapons were introduced into the reconnaissance detachments, which significantly increased the combat power of the units, and thus their capabilities.

Initially the le PzSpWg was built in two versions: the SdKfz 223 radio vehicle, recognizable by the foldable frame-type antenna, and the SdKfz 221 armed with a 7.92mm *Maschinengewehr* (MG – machine gun) 34.

Motorized Reconnaissance

1

As modern warfare has changed the nature of armed conflict, reconnaissance (both operational and tactical) has been given ever-increasing importance.

Essential decisions, such as the location or timing of a military operation, required good preparation. The same was true for any unit in the field exposed to the danger of a surprise and potentially devastating attack.

In the mid-1700s, Hussars came to be used as light cavalry in almost every army in Europe. Their superior speed meant that they were regularly used for reconnaissance. When led by intelligent and determined leaders, Hussars were also expected to fulfill limited combat missions, for example, disrupting enemy lines of supply or performing surprise attacks into their rear positions.

These cavalry units can, with some reservations, be considered as the forerunners of modern tactical reconnaissance. After the Napoleonic Wars, the Hussars were absorbed into a largely standardized cavalry. In many armies of Europe, the regiments were to be nominally preserved with their original names as part of maintaining tradition.

The Hussar regiments, like the Dragoon regiments, were now combat troops equipped with rifles, capable of fulfilling a wide variety of missions. In Germany, first to be assigned to infantry divisions in squadron (company) strength as dedicated reconnaissance units during the Franco-Prussian War (1870–1871). Even then, there was always the danger that army commanders would use the strong mobile units as mounted infantry and quickly wear them out.

The combat value of cavalry tasked with reconnaissance is indisputable. In the early 1900s, technical progress was to have a slow but lasting influence on the general conditions and operational principles of the troops. In the United States of America, Great Britain and Austria, reconnaissance units were

Opposite: In the 1920s, the *Reichswehr* began to receive a small number of wheeled personnel carriers. These unarmoured vehicles (SdKfz 3) were assigned to the newly formed *Kraftfahr-Abteilungen* (KfzAbt – motorized battalions) and used for troops to learn the battlefield tactics to be employed by a mobile army. But, despite having all-wheel drive, the SdKfz 3 had very limited off-road performance.

In World War I, tactical reconnaissance was still the task of horse-mounted units; the Hussars were considered to be the specialists. But the deployment of such a unit on what became a static battlefront made little sense.

equipped with motor vehicles for the first time; some were already armoured and equipped with light weapons.

In the German Reich, the influence of a conservative and, in many ways, backward general staff initially prevailed. Changes, such as the introduction of the motor vehicle, were implemented with significant hesitancy. This was noticed at the beginning of World War I, when cars and trucks were used mainly for the transport of supplies or as tractors for the increasingly heavy artillery. But this was to change as the war progressed. Both Great Britain and France invested large resources in the introduction of gun-mounted armoured vehicles. Whereas, the German Reich lacking finance and industrial resources was slow to respond.

After the end of the war, any momentum in Germany was slowed due to the strict restrictions imposed on the Reich under the terms of the Treaty of Versailles. These were demanded by France in particular, in order to weaken the former enemy decisively and for the long term. The restrictions outlawed the possession of heavy weaponry and prohibitied any development work; this was also applied to not only warships, but also tanks and wheeled armoured vehicles. The '100,000-man army' was only allowed a total of 100 obsolete machine-gun carrying armoured cars to equip the seven *Kraftfahr-Abteilungen* (KfAbt – motor battalions). These vehicles, built by various manufacturers, were only suitable for police duties since they were not designed to be cross-country capable. During the fight against the radical left-wing uprisings in Germany from 1919 to 1920, these armoured vehicles proved to be of great value despite their limitations. However, these vehicles did not meet the requirements of later military conflict. In the 1920s and 1930s, many essential tasks in the German army, including reconnaissance, would continue to be performed by horse-mounted units.

Despite the obvious technical disadvantages of the early armoured cars, Daimler-Benz was to develop a *'gepanzerter Kraftwagen für Mannschaftsbeförderung'* (armoured motor vehicle for personnel transport) in 1927 and build it in limited numbers (20 to 40 depending on the source). These were standardized as *Sonderkraftfahrzeug* (SdKfz – special-purpose vehicle) 3 and built on a simple two-axle chassis with all-wheel drive and solid rubber tyres. Designated as a *Mannschafts-Transportwagen* (MTW – personnel carrier), the large, lightly armoured vehicle could carry of up to 14 troops, but no armament.

The SdKfz 3 still served in the provisional motorized divisions in the first year of World War II and was recognizable by the large frame-type antenna for the two-way radio equipment.

Of similar design was the *Sonderwagen* (special vehicle) – known as the 'SchuPo' – produced for the *Schutz-Polizei* (security police) and built by Daimler

During the 1930s, there were three cavalry divisions, and all carefully nurtured and retained their traditions. With the build-up of the *Wehrmacht*, they were to be absorbed into other units with 3rd *Kavellerie Division* (3.KavDiv – cavalry division) forming the core of 1st Panzer Division (1.PzDiv).

as the DVRZ 21; Benz/21 (VP21) and the Ehrhardt/21. Unlike the *Kraftfahrzeug* (Kfz – motor vehicle) 3 the type had two rotatable turrets, each mounting a 7.92mm *Maschinengewehr* (MG – machine gun) 08/15, positioned on the top of the superstructure. It is thought that some 55 entered service in the 1920s, but all had been phased out by 1936.

The Cavalry in the 1930s

In *Reichswehr* (realm defence) times, three *Kavallerie Divisionen* (KavDiv – cavalry divisions) existed: 1.KavDiv; 2.KavDiv and 3.KavDiv. Towards the end of the 1920s, these were more or less equivalent to mounted infantry divisions, and yet retained their peacetime traditions. Nevertheless, the mounted regiments were soon assigned to other uses. Later, 3.KavDiv was to form almost the entire core of 1st Panzer Division (1.PzDiv). Finally, the command staffs of all cavalry divisions were disbanded in April 1936, and regiments, detachments, and squadrons were to be assigned to other duties.

It should be noted that this was not the end of all historic mounted units in the *Wehrmacht*. As late as October 1939, the 1st *Kavallerie-Brigade* (1.KavBde) was transformed into the new 1.KavDiv, which was to be deployed in Holland and then France during *Fall Gelb* (Plan Yellow) in 1940. The brigade also marched into the Soviet Union in June 1941. Here the large horse-mounted unit finally reached its limits. In December, it was withdrawn from the front and reorganized as 24.PzDiv. But in 1945, another two cavalry divisions (3.KavDiv and 4.KavDiv) were formed in Hungary.

Interestingly, the question of the necessity of mobile reconnaissance was, at the time, controversial. Under the impression of the experiences of trench warfare with static frontlines, often actually unchanging for months or even longer, leading military officers considered tactical reconnaissance to be ineffective and therefore irrelevant. However, this contradicted the views of most military theorists, who devised tactics to break through these fronts. In this context, it can be noted that, despite these considerations, France decided in the late 1920s to strengthen its eastern border by constructing a line of heavily-armed fortified defences, later known as the Maginot Line. Here, the advocates of static warfare had prevailed.

On the other hand, the then *Oberstleutnant* Heinz Guderian, the most prominent advocate of motorized forces along with *Generalmajor* Oswald Lutz, continued to emphasize the importance of mobile reconnaissance. Those apologists of modern mobile warfare called for cross-country-capable vehicles for the modern Hussars, whose reconnaissance results would provide military leaders with the prerequisites for long-range attack operations by armoured formations. As an ultimate goal, Guderian called for gun-mounted armoured

cars with the highest possible mobility on roads and also cross country.

Guderian (later *General der Panzertruppe*), who took over command of the *Panzerschule* (tank school) KAMA at Kazan (Soviet Union) in 1932, decided to almost divide his armoured force into two groups; those for reconnaissance and those to fight. The fact that these were given such prominence with little regard for the other subunits (artillery, etc.) underscores the great importance he attached to the reconnaissance units.

In 1936, Guderian formulated his demands in the *Militärwissenschaftliche Rundschau* (Military Scientific Review):

> For reconnaissance, particularly fast, agile, easy-to-lead units with a large radius of action and good intelligence means are needed. They have to see a lot and report without being observed. Therefore, the smaller they are the easier they are to conceal, which allows them to operate more effectively. Their firepower must be such that they can defend against or defeat a similarly armed enemy. If their mission requires more firepower, it must be supplied on a case-by-case basis.

Based on his experiences during visits abroad to observe foreign reconnaissance formations, he was completely aware of the equipment and vehicles used by other armies. His article continues:

> Heavy armoured reconnaissance vehicles are the carriers of modern ground reconnaissance. In most armies, wheeled vehicles are used for these tasks. They mainly use the roads, but have a certain off-road capability due to the installation of three or more axles and multi-wheel drive. Mechanical progress in the field of off-road vehicles has been considerable in recent years and development is promising. The maximum

For lack of suitable equipment, dummy tanks had to be used in the build-up phase of the new German armed forces. These simple non-armoured vehicles replicated all types of armoured vehicle.

Back in the days of the *Reichswehr*, large numbers of commercially available motor vehicles were utilized to train the troops. This BMW 3/15 'Dixi' – a licence-built Austin 7 – served as a Kfz 2, light telephone communication vehicle.

speed of these vehicles is between 70kph and 100kph, and their operating range is between 200km and 300km. Armament consists of machine guns and, in many cases, 2cm to 3.7cm anti-tank weapons. The armour is bound by weight limits due to the requirement for speed it must, at least, provide protection against infantry ammunition.

Operational Reconnaissance

After the first exercises by the *Kampfwagen-Nachbildungs-Bataillone* (dummy tank battalions) stationed at Grafenwöhr and Jüterbog in 1932, *Inspekteur der Kraftfahrtruppen* (In d KfTrp – inspector of mobile troops [later *Panzertruppe*]) 6 gave detailed thought to the importance of a reconnaissance element in the later tank divisions:

> The necessity of a platoon of small combat vehicles for the staff of a tank battalion is proven. It is indispensable for battalion reconnaissance activities as well as for liaison with the companies and with other sections of the armed forces during combat. Its temporary composition was assembled from the stocks held by the small combat vehicle platoons of the companies. But as it was observed during exercises, this must be considered as a stopgap measure. The companies need them to effectively perform their tasks. Difficulties in this regard arose especially on the training grounds at Grafenwöhr.

In early November 1932, the inspectorate really focused on the need for reconnaissance elements:

Approach and conduct of motorized reconnaissance

The use of motorized patrols should be ordered sparingly, otherwise the forces could become ineffective and unable to perform their duty. Their strength should be limited to what is necessary for a given task. The speed of our motor vehicles allows us to deploy fewer. Replacement of patrols as well as the deployment of new operations for less sensitive tasks must in all cases be from the reconnaissance reserve.

This approach to motorized reconnaissance makes more sense than deployment on the flank of an attack for the following reasons:

- A coordinated approach is ensured.
- The radio traffic between tank companies can be avoided.
- Unified command and control of the reconnaissance area is ensured.
- The retention of an effective reconnaissance reserve is possible.

The patrols for motorized reconnaissance will mostly be drawn from a tank company. Since the commander's vehicle will have radio equipment (*) he will be responsible not only for directing their actions, but also for evaluating operational reports received before transmitting them to the division commander.

All patrols should be assembled by using the minimum number of vehicles and only those most suited to the task. In the case of a road patrol by tanks, a group of four has proven to be too many, particularly in our territory. A patrol performed by two tanks is considered to be adequate. (**)

A reconnaissance patrol as part of a mixed (***) tank company: The heavy platoon (which can operate three separate patrols) is often deployed with the elements leading an attack. Here their heavy armour protection and powerful armament allows close observation of the enemy.

The division following will then use these preliminary observations and deliver them to the light platoon in preparation for further patrols by armoured companies to consolidate reconnaissance coverage. Motorcycle patrols can also be deployed for reconnaissance, especially to observe specific areas on the battlefront.

Mixed patrols, two *Panzerkampfwagen* (PzKpfw – tanks) and some light armoured MG-armed motor vehicles, have proved their worth in the exercises. This composition is particularly suitable to observe recognized enemy positions, since the light vehicles are more manoeuvrable and easier to conceal in the terrain.

The addition of *KradSchützen* [KradSchtz – motorcycle riflemen] to the reconnaissance division (mot), especially when the advance is being made on a road, has proven to be practical, since they can clear roadblocks more quickly and easily deal with small squads of enemy defenders.

It is essential that any town or village which is to be used as a base for patrols must be free of all enemy forces.

Standing patrols by PzKpfw reinforced or even completely replaced by KradSchtz. This is advantageous when awaiting a supply of fuel, essential vehicle maintenance, or to allow exhausted tank crews to recover after a long drive in their poorly ventilated vehicles.

Patrol leaders must always be fully briefed on their mission, particularly the last known location of enemy forces, and the position other patrols operating nearby.

Only in exceptional circumstances will the leader of a reconnaissance division (mot) have a completely clear picture of the enemy situation. Therefore, it is essential he remains at all times tactically alert and prepared for the unexpected.

In a situation where a patrol cannot move forward, the rapid deployment of the

Motorcycles were also procured in large quantities and were used for a variety of purposes. This NSU 501 TS with sidecar retains civilian number plates and is in service with the *Nationalsozialistisches Kraftfahrkorps* (NSKK). The troop affiliation of the soldiers cannot be determined with certainty.

entire battalion can often cause the enemy to fall back. But it must be clear that such action has a limited objective.

Although combat in general is not the province of motorized reconnaissance detachments, any good opportunity for a surprise attack must not be missed.

I expect this will become an everyday occurrence once our reconnaissance forces gain more experience on the battlefront.

(*) In 1932, radios were available only in small numbers.
(**) Later the patrol would typically be assembled by the reconnaissance leader on a task-by-task basis.
(***) The mixed tank company was issued with both 3.7cm-armed PzKpfw III and 7.5cm KwK 37 L/24-armed PzKpfw IV.

The report makes clear that Guderian expected his reconnaissance units to fulfill limited combat missions or to offer holding resistance. At the same time, he recognized that in addition to the reconnaissance detachments working in

This BMW 3/15 Dixi has been slightly modified for use in the *Reichswehr*. For example, the windscreen has been painted to simulate the restricted field of vision when driving an armoured car.

The SchuPo SW was introduced after the end of World War I. The large armoured vehicle carried two small turrets with each mounting a water-cooled machine gun. The type was unsuitable for use as a reconnaissance vehicle. (Getty)

Above: In 1927, Büssing-NAG developed the futuristic-looking *Zehnradwagen* (ZRW – ten-wheel vehicle). It was steered like a tracked vehicle: to negotiate a bend, the brakes had to be applied to the wheels on one side, which resulted in unacceptable wear on tyres and linings.

Right: The ZRW was designed to be amphibious, but to increase buoyancy cork floats were attached to the sides of the superstructure.

isolation, the commanders of the tank regiments and detachments needed their own active reconnaissance elements during combat.

At this point, Guderian does not go into detail. Neither were the tasks of the reconnaissance division specified, nor did he confirm the necessary joint arrangements between the *Aufklärungs-Abteilungen* (*motorisiert*) (AufklAbt [mot] – reconnaissance battalions [motorized]) and combat troops.

Six months later, the exact composition of the latter was still not clearly defined. In an essay dated 3 August 1933, which dealt with the timetable for the expansion of the *Panzertruppe* (tank force), Guderian clarifies his opinion for this new type of force:

Expansion of the Panzertruppe

The numerical inferiority imposed on us by the Treaty makes even a defensive war almost hopeless. I believe, however, that I must make suggestions as to what possibilities arise from the exploitation of motorization. At the top of the list is the demand for operational mobility, primarily because this can compensate for numerical inferiority. Only operational mobility guarantees freedom of action; since it offers – in view of the current situation in Germany – the only prospect of success.

This operational mobility, in addition to the full utilization of the rail network and road transport, can only be achieved by rapidly moving combat units. These are to be deployed, independently from other units, rapidly and in large numbers, to strike deep into the flanks and rear positions of an enemy.

The cavalry can no longer fulfill this task; it is not a fast-moving force in the operational sense. It is more or less a mounted infantry.

The prerequisite for operational agility is that our commanders receive the necessary information to allow timely strategic decisions to be made. This is the role of operational reconnaissance and can only be achieved by deploying motorized units in the field, often cooperating with *Luftwaffe* reconnaissance units.

These reconnaissance detachments, which are of essential importance for the deployment of armoured units, are already to some extent existant. A review of these units in light of my above comments is desirable. Their final composition still depends on further experience.

Expansion of the motorized reconnaissance battalions

Although we have gained much experience, more is required. A distinction will have to be made between:

a.) Operational long-range reconnaissance at the disposal of the army command.

b.) Reconnaissance detachments for armoured units and light divisions.

A commercially available truck has been fitted with a superstructure, fabricated from wood and canvas, which replicates an 'enemy' armoured vehicle. Many of these were used during *Reichswehr* exercises where troops were training for armoured warfare.

c.) Tactical reconnaissance detachments for cavalry divisions.

The reconnaissance battalion for (a) and (b) will have approximately the same strength:

- Staff with signals platoon.
- Two tank companies.
- Two motorcycle companies.
- A heavy company with an anti-tank, and infantry guns supported by an engineer squad.

The reconnaissance detachments as in (c) may be considerably weaker, such as a mixed company of tanks and motorcycle troops. The requirement for reconnaissance detachments such as (a) and (b) has so far been fixed at 12, but this number will have to be reviewed. These reconnaissance units, like the tank units, must be ready for deployment in the shortest possible time and initially have the same strength as peacetime units.

Proposal: Deployment of two PzKpfw and two heavy companies each year until the seven KfAbt are brought up to the strength of two PzKpfw and one heavy company.

This structure for the AufklAbt was to be adopted in principle. The core of the later *Panzertruppe* with all subunits was formed by the seven KfAbt from the days of the *Reichswehr*. On 1 May 1933, these were renamed

Kraftfahr-Kampf-Abteilungen (KfKpfAbt – motor armoured battalions). Due to lack of equipment in October 1934, these divisions consisted of 14 *Kampfwagen-Abwehr-Abteilungen* (tank destroyer battalions) as well as seven AufklAbt (mot).

Note, the designation *Kampfwagen* (Kpfw – tank) and Panzer (Pz) were both used at that time.

The seven KfAbt were consolidated under the command of a *Kraftfahr-Kavallerie Korps* (KfKavKps – vehicle-mounted cavalry), each having an AufklAbt and two PzAbwAbt. The AufklAbt were deployed as follows:

- KfAbt 1 with AufklAbt 1 in Königsberg
- KfAbt 2 with AufklAbt 2 in Stettin
- KfAbt 3 with AufklAbt 3 in Wünsdorf
- KfAbt 4 with AufklAbt 4 in Königsberg
- KfAbt 5 with AufklAbt 5 in Stuttgart
- KfAbt 6 with AufklAbt 6 in Münster
- KfAbt 7 with AufklAbt 7 in München

A further three reconnaissance units were raised in regimental strength, reinforced by cavalry, and were later assigned to the light divisions. The first Panzer divisions, 1.PzDiv, 2.PzDiv and 3.PzDiv, were formed in October 1935.

In 1927, Daimler-Benz delivered the prototype of their design for an *Achtradwagen* (ARW – eight-wheel vehicle). The type had all-wheel drive and was armed with two 7.92mm 08/15 machine guns mounted in the small conical turret.

As early as the mid-1920s, the newly created *Heereswaffenamt* (HWA – army ordnance office) was preparing the specifications for wheeled all-terrain armoured vehicles. This apparent contravention of the provisions of the Treaty of Versailles should not be surprising, since the restrictions were considered unjust and disgraceful not only by the Reich government but also members of the public. Those intent on rebuilding the military sought to circumvent them wherever possible or to interpret them generously.

The Military Inter-Allied Commission of Control monitored German compliance with the military provisions of the Treaty, and carried out inspections of all military installations and reported back to the Allied governments. The German Reich had to pay the costs for all of the inspections.

Under the Paris Agreement dated 31 January 1927, the Commission ceased its work on 1 February 1927. Arms control in Germany was now the responsibility of the League of Nations, which the German Reich had joined on 10 September, 1926, after signing the Locarno Agreements. During the period of its activity, the Commission carried out more than 33,000 inspections, equivalent to some 28 missions per day. Under its supervision, some 6,000,000 infantry rifles, 105,000 machine guns, 28,470 mortars and replacement barrels, 54,887 guns and replacement barrels, 38,750,000 artillery shells, and 490,000,000 rounds of infantry ammunition were destroyed, as well as 14,014 aircraft, 27,757 aircraft engines, 31 armoured trains and 59 tanks. The destruction of this equipment was carried out according to the regulations by the German Reich, and were supervised by Allied control officers.

In the mid-1920s, the HWA had completed work on the specifications for wheeled armoured vehicles and secret development contracts were awarded to major German manufacturers. The requirements were ambitious, pushing

Opposite: An Adler-built Kfz 13 during a *Reichswehr* exercise: the rear-wheel-drive vehicles were lightly armoured and carried a single 7.92mm MG 13 fitted on a pedestal-type mounting, behind the driver, in the fighting compartment. The vehicle commander also functioned as the gunner.

In 1935, Büssing-NAG delivered the first prototype for the specified eight-wheel reconnaissance vehicle. This experimental chassis was fitted with independent suspension and mechanically complicated all-wheel steering, which would be used on later vehicles.

the limits of what was technically feasible. Instead of using the chassis of conventional passenger cars or trucks, targeted designs were required. In order to distribute the weight of the combat vehicles as evenly as possible, they had to be designed with multi-wheel drive, emphasizing the requirement for all-terrain mobility

Fitted with permanent all-wheel drive, the vehicles had to be as agile as possible on hard-surfaced roads, and also be capable of climbing an obstacle and crossing a ditch. The specified maximum speed was to be 65kph and mechanically, the type had to be sufficiently reliable to cover 200km on each of three consecutive days at an average speed of 30kph. The original specification also demanded that the type must be capable of being driven forward or reverse at equally high speeds, most advantageous in certain combat situations. In the event of being discovered by the enemy, the armoured reconnaissance vehicle could immediately escape in reverse without having to perform a time-consuming turning manoeuvre.

The vehicles were designed to be buoyant to allow water obstacles, such as a lake or wide river, to be crossed. The wheeled types were to have most effective armament available, and a 3.7cm gun was to be mounted in a turret. The armour was adequate to protect against fire from 7.92mm *Spitzgeschoss* standard infantry ammunition.

In 1927, Daimler-Benz and Magirus each supplied designs of an *Achtradwagen* (ARW – eight-wheel vehicle) while Büssing-NAG completed design work on their *Zehnradwagen* (ZRW – ten-wheel vehicle). These developments were also known by the general camouflage designation *Mannschafts-Transportwagen*. While the eight-wheel types had two steered axles – one at the front and one rear – the ZRW was steered, similar to a tank, by applying the brakes to five wheels on one side. Although this method was simple, and saved interior space, it proved to be impractical due to heavier than expected tyre wear and also expensive time-consuming maintenance of components in the braking system.

These extremely advanced vehicles, many of which were revolutionary, were tested extensively between 1930 and 1931, some at Kazan. The tests proved successful, but the vehicles were too expensive to build and did not progress beyond the prototype and pre-production stages. Subsequently, none were delivered to combat units.

Initial Equipment

By the end of the 1920s, the German Reich had almost completed the somewhat uncompromising expansion of its armed forces. In the process, the restrictions of the Treaty of Versailles were circumvented with increasing carelessness. Nevertheless, development work, especially on armoured vehicles and their testing, still had to take place in secret. The Treaty of Rapallo in 1922, saw Germany enter a period of close cooperation with the Soviet Union, which allowed the first elements of what would become the *Panzerwaffe* and *Luftwaffe* to be trained in secret at KAZAN and Lipetsk. However, this presumably mutually beneficial arrangement ended after Hitler seized power in 1933.

A *Maschinengewehr-Kraftwagen* (machine-gun vehicle [Kfz13]), armed with a 7.92mm MG 13 on a pedestal mount, and a *Funkkraftwagen* (Kfz 14) being prepared for duty. The Kfz 14 carried a 5W transceiver and a frame-type antenna which would be erected to operate the radio.

Above: Adler-built armoured cars were used for the first time under wartime conditions during the occupation of Czechoslovakia. Here a Kfz 14 radio car and two Kfz 13 MG cars enter the capital, Prague.

Right: The Kfz 13 utilized either the standard medium passenger car chassis of a Daimler-Benz 10/50hp or an Adler 12/55hp. Front armour on the Kfz 13 was impenetrable from 7.92mm *Spitzgeschoss mit Kern* (SmK – armour-piercing ammunition), and the sides were safe against standard 7.92mm infantry ammunition.

The proposed rapid equipping of the *Reichswehr* with modern weaponry was limited by the constraints placed on financial resources. The problem was further exacerbated by an armaments industry ill-prepared to increase production, and the ongoing shortage of important raw materials. Priority was being given to the production of large numbers of PzKpfw I to equip the new Panzer divisions. Consequently, this also delayed many other projects.

The creation of the effective reconnaissance units that Guderian had in mind occurred under the worst possible circumstances. Suitable armoured vehicles were not available, and so the only option was to equip them with conventional motor vehicles. In 1929, the inspectorate of cavalry had ordered trials with a motorized squadron as part of *Reiter-Regiment* (horse regiment) 4 at Potsdam. Further details are not known, but it is likely that commercial light passenger cars, thought to be suitable for training the troops, were used. This made it possible for the units involved to develop initial operational tactics.

Initially, the BMW Dixi – a licence-built Austin 7 – light motor car was selected to be partially militarized for use for light reconnaissance duties. Some were fitted with a fabricated armour shield in place of the conventional windscreen. In the early 1930s, the same vehicle type was often covered with a canvas and wood body for use as a dummy tank for training recruits to the armoured force.

Even before the war began, the 7.92mm MG 13 was replaced by the more effective 7.92mm MG 34, which had an increased rate of fire, was simpler to operate and proved more reliable in battle.

Above: In response to the demand made by the *Waffenamt* (weapons office) for a heavy armoured reconnaissance vehicle, the chassis of various commercially available trucks were fitted with an all-round sloping armoured superstructure and a dummy turret.

Right: The 6-Rad specification called for both a front and a rear driver. Access to the rear driving position was through a large tailgate.

Left: Small domes were fitted over both driving positions. They would be opened to provide better visibility, but be firmly closed in action.

Below: A production version of the s PzSpWg (6-Rad). In addition to a 7.92mm MG 13, a 2cm *Kampfwagenkanone* (KwK – tank gun) 30 was now mounted in the turret, significantly improving firepower.

Basically, two combat vehicles were required for the reconnaissance units:

- A light armoured scout car armed with machine guns, or with radio equipment.
- A larger type to carry out more varied combat missions as a heavy armoured reconnaissance vehicle. For this purpose, it was decided to equip it with a 2cm *Kampfwagenkanone* (KwK – tank gun) 30 L/55 cannon and machine guns. A variant with powerful radio equipment was also planned.

Effective communications were given high priority at an early stage. The development of high-performance radios for installation in armoured vehicles was given high priority. Major problems arose in the field: vibration, moisture, dirt and variations in temperature all impacted performance. One serious problem was the suppression of interference from the ignition and other electrical items in the vehicle.

Initially, while work on the above problems continued, only the vehicles issued to staff at company commander and above were equipped with a radio; all others depended on flag or flare-gun signals. One possible reason for this may have been the insufficient capacity of German industry.

Before specialized and more powerful armoured reconnaissance vehicles were available, temporary solutions were introduced.

The PzSpWg RK 9 was developed in Austria by Saurer, a company which had vast experience in building wheel-cum-track vehicles. Their design combined high road speeds with good off-road capability, but because of high production costs only a relatively small number were built.

The Austrian-built RK 9 was powered by a 100hp Saurer OKD four-cylinder diesel engine.

Kfz 13 and Kfz 14

Both Daimler-Benz and Adler had supplied the *Heer* (army) with motor vehicles that were used for a wide variety of purposes. These rear-wheel-drive vehicles were fitted with large diameter wheels which resulted in a high ground clearance. In 1933, a first armoured car was produced by utilizing one such chassis and featured a simple open-topped armoured superstructure built round the passenger compartment, which provided protection against fire from 7.92mm infantry ammunition. The engine-cooling radiator was protected by a thicker plate that was safe against 7.92mm *Spitzgeschoss mit Kern* (SmK – armour-piercing ammunition). However, the engine bay was not armoured. The vehicle, which weighed 2,000kg, was powered by a 50hp petrol engine which allowed a top speed of some 70kph to be reached.

Two variants were delivered: a *Maschinengewehr-Kraftwagen* (machine-gun vehicle [Kfz 13]) which mounted a single 7.92mm MG 13, and an unarmed *Funkkraftwagen* (radio vehicle [Kfz 14]) which carried a *Funkgeräte* (Fu – radio device) 9 SE 5. This consisted of a 5W Sender (S – transmitter) linked to a *Rahmenantenne* (frame-type aerial) which allowed an operational range of 20km (voice), 50km (Morse). A receiving set, the *Tornister-Empfänger* (TornEmpf – portable transceiver) 'b', was available. This was the equipment of the small radio squad 'b', and provided a two-way link. Although built with high ground clearance, the off-road mobility of the heavy vehicles was poor, since they lacked four-wheel drive. The troops called these vehicles *'Badewanne'* (bathtub).

Three s PzSpWg (Fu)
(6-Rad) on parade.
The two outer vehicles
were built by Magirus
and between them is a
Büssing-NAG type. (Getty)

Kfz 67 and Kfz 67a

In 1930, the army began receiving a new type of light off-road *Lastkraftwagen* (truck) which utilized the three-axle chassis of a standard 1,500kg-capacity commercial vehicle. Daimler-Benz supplied the G 3a, Büssing-NAG the *Typ* G31, followed later by Magirus with the *Typ* M 206. Mechanically these vehicles were very similar with only the two rear axles being driven and were produced in a wide variety of variants for the military.

The HWA issued a request to the three companies to design an economical 'wheeled tank' on a truck chassis. To achieve this the chassis had to be lengthened, and a radically angled armoured superstructure, the first of which were supplied by Deutsche Werke, fitted. The distinctive 'coffin' shape was to be adopted for all later German armoured reconnaissance vehicles, and also infantry fighting vehicles. The angled armour – 14.5mm (front) and 8mm (side) – was impervious to 7.92mm armour-piercing infantry ammunition. The first vehicles were tested in 1932.

The Magirus chassis was powered by a six-cylinder S 88 engine; the Daimler-Benz by the M 09 six-cylinder engine; and the Bussing-NAG by a Type G four-cylinder engine. All were liquid cooled and petrol fuelled. Although engine power differed, the vehicle weight – some 6,000kg – was identical across all models, as was the

The SdKfz 221 light armoured reconnaissance vehicle was similar in concept to the Kfz 13. The white *Balkenkreuz*, introduced in 1939, does not refer to the Balkans but to a cross made of two heavy timbers.

The Steyr-built ADGZ entered service with the Austrian army in 1935 as an armoured car for police duties. The vehicle was armed with a 20mm cannon and two to three machine guns. After the *Anschluss*, German forces deployed the few available vehicles to fight partisans.

maximum speed of 70kph. A rotatable turret, mounting a 2cm KwK 30 L/55 and an MG 13, was positioned on the rear of the superstructure.

Initially the vehicles were designated Kfz 67, but in early 1936 they were classified as *schwerer Panzerspähwagen (Sechsrad)* (s PzSpWg [6-Rad] – heavy armoured car [six-wheel]) and designated SdKfz 231. When the type first entered front-line service, none were fitted with radio equipment.

Additionally, a variant was built as a *schwerer Panzerspähwagen* (Funk) (s PzSpWg [Fu] – heavy armoured car [radio]) and was initially designated as the *Kraftfahrzeug* (Kfz – motor vehicle) 67a, but from 1936 it was classified as the SdKfz 232. These vehicles were equipped with the long-range radio which was used by the *mittlerer Funktrupp* (medium radio squad) 'b', and also reconnaissance and the signals units. The Fu 11 equipment consisted of a 100W *Sender* (S – transmitter) and the TornEmpf 'b'. To achieve the maximum range of 70km (voice) and 200km (Morse), a 9m *Kurbelmast* (telescopic mast) fitted with a *Sternantenne* (star antenna) 'a' was normally used. However, all SdKfz 232 were only equipped with a large *Rahmenantenne*, which probably resulted in much shorter ranges.

In order to fully exploit the possibilities of radio technology, specialized *Panzerfunkwagen* (armoured radio vehicles) were introduced. At the end

In 1941, an unknown
number of SdKfz 221
were converted to
mount a 2.8cm *schwere
Panzerbüchse*
(s PzB – heavy anti-tank
rifle) 41, as an attempt
to improve anti-tank
defence for a *Panzerspär-
Kompanie* (PzSpKp –
armoured reconnaissance
company). However,
the effectiveness of this
weapon had already
been acknowledged as
doubtful.

of 1935, the first tranche of 12 heavy armoured scout cars (Kfz 67a) were
converted. The rotatable turret and the 2cm KwK main gun were removed
and replaced with a fixed extension to the superstructure. The only armament
carried was an MG 13 machine gun for self-defence which was mounted in the
front of the new superstructure. Again, the Fu 11 radio was installed, but the
9m *Kurbelmast* was mounted inside the vehicle. Initially, all were designated
as *Panzerfunkwagen* (Kfz 67b), but later were classified as the SdKfz 263. The
few vehicles available were assigned to the *Panzer-Nachrichten-Abteilungen*
(PzNachrAbt – armoured signals battalion) and to *Panzer-Nachrichten-Zug*
(PzNachrZg – armoured signals platoon) of the AufklAbt (mot) in each PzDiv.
The chassis of the heavy armoured reconnaissance vehicle was overloaded by
the armoured superstructure. Driving performance was not satisfactory on
paved roads or off-road.

Modern Types

Even before the first Panzer divisions were formed, the HWA had demanded
wheeled armoured vehicles, but now it issued orders for vehicles with excellent
off-road mobility to gradually replace the early six-wheel types and equip the
reconnaissance units for modern warfare. These new light and heavy armoured
reconnaissance vehicles were purpose designed and specialized variants would
be produced in to meet any challenge.

The SdKfz 222 was much better armed than the earlier SdKfz 221. The vehicle was armed with a coaxially mounted 2cm KwK 30 L/55 and MG 34 on a *Sockellafette* (pedestal mount). A flat rotatable turret – in reality this was no more than an all-round armoured shield – was mounted on the superstructure, which had been widened to accommodate a three-man crew.

The coaxially mounted 2cm KwK 30 L/55 – later vehicles had the 2cm KwK 38 L/55 and MG 34.

Light Armoured Scout Car

Starting in 1935, a *leichter Panzerspähwagen* (le PzSpWg – light armoured scout car) was developed on the chassis of the *Einheitsfahrgestell für schwere Personenkraftwagen* (standard chassis for heavy passenger cars) that had been in production since 1934. This chassis with four-wheel drive was being built by Horch as the Type 801 and used in modified form for the Kfz 69 *Protzkraftwagen* (prime mover vehicle [gun tractor]) and also an MTW (Kfz 70), among others.

The two-axle chassis of the le PzSpWg had an over-elaborate independent coil-sprung suspension. Both axles were driven and steerable. For driving at speeds above 25kph, but to ensure safety the driver had to lock the rear steering since the type could easily overturn.

The chassis was initially produced as *Ausführung* (Ausf – model/mark) Ausf A, and powered by a 3,500cc Horch V-8 petrol engine. Later, a reinforced chassis with a 3,800cc engine went into production as the Ausf B. The two-part superstructure was fabricated from 5.5mm to 8mm thick heavily sloped armour plates and was safe against 7.92mm SmK armour-piercing infantry ammunition from range of 30m.

These vehicles were initially intended to support Kfz 13 and Kfz 14 and later replace them completely. The le PzSpWg was produced in five variants

The SdKfz 223 (Fu) was used for communications with the higher command echelons of the AufklAbt. Initially, the vehicles were equipped with a long-range 30W (S – transmitter) and a frame-type antenna. Note, the SdKfz 223 is still equipped with a 7.92mm MG 13.

which, depending on purpose and armament, differed slightly in the shape of the armoured superstructure.

SdKfz 221

The le PzSpWg (MG) was standardized as the SdKfz 221, but in fact it was nothing more than an improved Kfz 13. The vehicle carried an MG 13 (later MG 34) on a pedestal-type mounting in the centre of the chassis and a crew of two. The gunner, who was also the commander of the vehicle, sat behind the weapon mounting. A *Panzerschild* (armoured shield) – in reality, a small open turret – was fitted but only gave him protection from shrapnel and light ammunition. If necessary, a third man could sit in the rear; to do this, a grille had to be raised behind the *Panzerschild*.

Initially, no radio was installed, which restricted the operational value of the vehicle. But beginning in 1941, a FuSprech 'a' transceiver began to be fitted in all production vehicles and field engineer units. A two-piece wire cover for the armoured shield was also fitted during final assembly. Production of the SdKfz 221 was terminated in 1940 after some 330 had been delivered.

The SdKfz 261, *kleiner Panzerfunkwagen* (kl PzFuWg – small armoured radio vehicle) was fitted with specialized radios, and were initially only assigned to *Nachrichten-Abteilungen* (NachrAbt – signals battalions). Unlike the SdKfz 223, these vehicles were not armed.

Right: The *Versuchs-Kraftfahrzeug* (VersKfz – prototype vehicle) 623 was the first version of the s PzSpWg (8-wheel). Initially, the type was fitted with a turret from a SdKfz 231 (6-Rad).

Below: Adolf Hitler inspects a VersKfz 623 during a military exercise. The vehicle has been fitted with a production-type turret.

SdKfz 222

A better armed light armoured scout car was developed in parallel to the SdKfz 221. Although it was basically similar in design, the SdKfz 222 had a wider superstructure. Initially this fabricated in two parts, but on later vehicles it was made in three parts. A 2cm KwK 30 L/55 and an MG 13 (replaced by the more modern MG 34 in 1938) were mounted on a *Sockellafette* (pedastal gun mount) 38 in the centre of the crew compartment. The vehicle carried a crew of three: a driver, the commander (who also operated the weapons) and a loader. The SdKfz 222 was relatively well armed for a reconnaissance vehicle, since the 2cm auto-cannon could also be used for defence against low-flying enemy aircraft.

The SdKfz 222 was also not equipped with radio until 1941. But as always, various minor changes and improvements were made during production, including the installation of a FuSprech 'a' in 1941. It is thought that some 1,000 of these vehicles were delivered between 1935 and 1943.

SdKfz 223 (Fu)

To provide the reconnaissance units with long-range radio communications, the le PzSpWg (Fu) was developed. The vehicle resembled the SdKfz 221, but had a wider armoured superstructure. An MG 13, operated by the vehicle driver was mounted for self-defence.

This early (1937) production s PzSpWg (8-Rad) is still painted in *Reichswehr* tri-colour *Buntfarben-Anstrich* (brightly coloured) camouflage.

Above: This early s PzSpWg (8-Rad) shows details of the engine ventilation and exhaust system. As the vehicles had a reverse driver, the lighting system was designed accordingly, it was even fitted with two horns. The frame on the side of the hull is a *Fliegerschwenkarm* (anti-aircraft swivel arm).

Right: The s PzSpWg (8-Rad) had all-wheel drive, all-wheel steering and independent suspension which gave the vehicle a high-degree of manoeuvrability.

The SdKfz 223 was initially equipped with a Fu 10 radio which featured a 30W transmitter and a TornEmpf 'b'. The transmitter allowed a maximum range of 90km (Morse) when using the 8m *Kurbelmast* fitted with *Sternantenne* 'a'. However, the SdKfz 223 was equipped with a fold-down, frame-type antenna. Additionally, a 5m-long antenna fitted with a *Sternantenne* 'a' was mounted next to the small turret.

From 1940, the Fu 10 was successively replaced by the more powerful Fu 12 equipment (S 'a' transmitter and E 'c' receiver). When operated with a frame-type antenna, a range of between 25km (voice) and 80km (Morse) was attainable.

Over 550 of the type were produced between 1935 and 1944.

Above: An s PzSpWg (8-Rad), in service with the *Panzer-AufKlarungs-Abteilung* (PzAufKl46t – armoured reconnaissance battalion) 4 (1.PzDiv), has been fitted with a *Zerscheller-Platte* (shatter plate) in an attempt to improve frontal protection. The practice began at the end of 1940, but it made the vehicle front heavy.

SdKfz 260 and SdKfz 261

Unarmed radio vehicles were also to be developed on the basic light armoured reconnaissance vehicle. Two variants of *Panzerfunkwagen* were introduced to carry a complete signals section:

The SdKfz 260 carried the *kleiner Funktrupp* (small radio squad) 'c' fitted with an Fu 7 radio; a 20W S 'd' transmitter and a high-frequency 'd' receiver. The radio was used for ground-to-air communications by the *Flieger-Verbindungsoffizier* (FliVO – air liaison officer) to maintain contact with

Luftwaffe units performing reconnaissance missions. In 1941, the short-range FuSprech 'a' also began to be installed in the type.

The SdKfz 261 carrying the *kleiner Funktrupp* 'd' was equipped with a Fu 12 radio (80W S 'a' transmitter and Mw E 'c' receiver) attached to a frame-type antenna. The short-range FuSprech 'a' radio began to be fitted in 1941.

Between April 1941 and April 1943, a total of 132 light armoured radio vehicles were produced. The SdKfz 260 and SdKfz 261 were assigned to the *Nachrichten-Abteilungen* (NachrAbt – signals battalions) in the Panzer divisions, but were normally issued to AufklAbt (mot).

Achtrad

At a meeting held in the early 1930s, *Inspektion* (department) 6 of the HWA announced that the new reconnaissance units were in urgent need of a heavy armoured reconnaissance vehicle. Basic experience was available, but the first multi-wheel prototypes had proven to be too mechanically complex and thus expensive to mass produce.

The heavy armoured reconnaissance vehicles (6-Rad) which used the chassis of commercially available trucks were intended from the outset as a temporary solution until more modern and more powerful equipment was available. The concept of the multi-wheeled vehicles was to be continued with production to set to begin in 1935 or 1936 at the latest.

The engineers responsible for development in the HWA examined other concepts during this period. For example, the wheel-cum-track vehicles developed in the inter-war period, which could run on wheels as well as tracks, seemed promising. The type was designed to combine high road speed travelling on wheels and the tracks for cross-country mobility or poor road conditions.

In Austria, the Saurer company had already initiated various projects in 1936. One, the RR-7 *Räder-Raupe* (*) (wheel-cum-track), was commandeered by German forces after the Anschluss and taken to the Reich where it was fitted with an armoured superstructure. By 1941 a total of 128, classified as the SdKfz 254, had been completed and all were issued to the artillery observation units of a PzArtAbt attached to a Panzer division. When the PzSpWg (6-Rad) was deemed to be obsolete and taken out of front-line service, the designation SdKfz 232 was transferred to the s PzSpWg 8-Rad (Fu).

At the beginning of 1938, the HWA directly contracted Saurer to develop an armoured reconnaissance vehicle based on their RK-9 (*Räder-Kette**) tractor. Daimler-Benz supplied a turret mounting a heavy tank gun and an MG 34. But during trials, major problem arose with the installation of the engine which caused the interior to become overheated. Nevertheless, an 0-series was ordered, but this was soon cancelled and none were ever built.

Opposite: The Büssing-NAG Type GS chassis was selected as the basis for a specialized *Panzerfunkwagen* (PzFuWg – armoured radio car). Instead of a turret, it was fitted with a fixed superstructure and a standard frame-type antenna. The type was designated as SdKfz 263 and was fitted with a 100W radio.

A group of *Wehrmacht* officers inspect a recently delivered SdKfz 263 (8-Rad).

(*) The terms *Raupe* (caterpillar) and *Kette* (track) were interchangeable. In German-speaking countries, the use of *Kette* soon became the norm.

Shortly before the start of the war, Hanomag also received an order to develop a heavy armoured reconnaissance vehicle utilizing their extensive half-track vehicle technology. The chassis used was similar to that of the SdKfz 11, but the engine was mounted at the rear. According to various sources, 30 of these chassis were built under the designation H 8 H and at least one was fitted with a tank-type superstructure and a turret. However, there is no evidence to suggest that this innovative design ever went into production.

In 1937, Büssing-NAG was finally able to deliver the first prototypes of its design for an *Achtradwagen*: the *Versuchs-Kraftfahrzeug* (VersKfz – prototype combat vehicle) 623 (*schwerer Panzerspähwagen*) and VersKfz 624 (*schwerer Panzerspähwagen* [Fu]).

The construction was technically demanding and complicated. Each axle was suspended by leaf springs mounted on a subframe bolted to the main chassis. A Bussing-NAG L8V liquid-cooled petrol engine was mounted on the rear of the chassis. The *Panzeraufbau* (armoured superstructure), was fabricated, as with previous armoured cars, from steeply angled plating. The complete assembly was bolted to the chassis, to improve overall rigidity.

The superstructure was fabricated in two parts from armour 5.5mm to 14.5mm thick, which protected the crew from infantry firing 7.92mm SmK ammunition. On the front part of the superstructure a closed turret was mounted. This carried the armament, a 2cm KwK 30 L/55 and an MG 34. The 150hp Büssing-NAG 8-cylinder engine allowed a maximum speed of 90kph. The rear third of the tank

The SdKfz 247 Ausf A, *gepanzerte Stäbewagen* (armoured staff car) was specially developed for reconnaissance battalions. But in 1941, a new variant [here], the SdKfz 247 Ausf B, was produced by Daimler-Benz using a two-axle *Einheitsfahrgestell* (standard chassis).

superstructure could be completely removed to allow good access to the engine for repair or replacement.

At the time of introduction the s PzSpWg (VersKfz 623), as in other German scout cars, was not fitted with a radio. The VersKfz 624 was equipped the same powerful Fu 11, which had a range of 70km (voice), 200km (Morse), once fitted in the SdKfz 232 (6-Rad). The vehicle carried frame-type antenna, mounted on insulating wooden rods, which covered the entire length of the vehicle.

After the completion of extensive trials, the new heavy armoured reconnaissance vehicles were respectively classified SdKfz 233 and SdKfz 234. But when the last of the 6-Rad type were withdrawn from active service, both were reclassified in September 1940; SdKfz 233 became SdKfz 231, and SdKfz 234 became SdKfz 232.

SdKfz 263

A variant based on the heavy armoured scout car (8-Rad) was also developed as a *Panzerfunkwagen*.

Instead of the rotatable turret, the armoured superstructure was enlarged upwards, to allow space for the equipment of the *mittlerer Panzer-Funktrupp* (m PzFuTrp – medium armoured signals section), the Fu 11 radio, was installed. Behind the superstructure the associated 9m *Kurbelmast* was also mounted, which operated with the *Sternantenne* 'a'. In addition, a frame antenna was available, thanks to which the radio could be operated while driving. To reach greater distances with the *Kurbelmast*, it had to be extended while stationary. These vehicles first entered service in 1938 as PzFuWg [SdKfz 263] and were assigned to the PzNachrAbt in each PzDiv and also to PzNachrZg of an AufklAbt (mot). Some 200 of the type had been delivered by 1943.

SdKfz 247

The lengthy designation *schwerer geländegängiger gepanzerter Personenkraftwagen* (s gl gep Pkw – heavy cross-country armoured personnel carrier) concealed an armoured command vehicle that was to be supplied exclusively to the staff of reconnaissance regiments and battalions. This served the commanders as a light armoured command vehicle.

A total of ten vehicles were assembled in 1937 on the three-axle chassis of the Krupp-built Kfz 69 and classified as the SdKfz 247 Ausf A. The open-topped bodywork was partially armoured and protected those inside from 7.92mm SmK ammunition. The vehicle was not fitted with any armament.

Surprisingly, these vehicles were not equipped with a radio, possibly an indication of a difficult supply situation which was to continue throughout the war. All were to be issued to AufklAbt (mot) and *Aufklärungs-Regimenter* (AufKlRgt – reconnaissance regiment).

In 1938, the HWA ordered the development of a second series. These vehicles were to utilize the two-axle *Einheits-Fahrgestell* II, manufactured by Horch. However, production, which began in July 1941, was carried out by Daimler-Benz and ended in January 1942 after 58 vehicles, designated SdKfz 247 Ausf B, had been delivered. Again, the vehicles were not fitted with radio equipment, nor were they armed.

In service, one vehicle would be issued to the staff section of a reconnaissance battalion and another to the staff of a motorcycle-mounted infantry battalion. From 1941, radio equipment began to be fitted as a standard item.

German troops enter Prague during the annexation of Czechoslovakia. Initially, the reconnaissance troops were equipped with large numbers of *Beiwagen-Kräder* (motorcycle and sidecar [combination]) until more armoured vehicles became available. (Getty)

Motorized Battalion

3

In January 1935, the timetable for the formation of the *Kraftfahrkampftruppe*, the later *Panzertruppen*, was set. Initially, three Panzer divisions were to be established by the end of the year.

The plan was to have all the necessary equipment available by the summer of 1935. However, the expansion of the armoured force proceeded with considerable disruption. Due to the dire economic situation and manufacturing difficulties, the initial equipment supplied varied widely. For example, 3.7cm and 7.5cm *Panzerkampfwagen* (the later PzKpfw III and PzKpfw IV) could not be introduced in the required numbers on schedule. As a result, improvisation was necessary and the deployment of the reconnaissance units was similarly chaotic.

The allocation of available reconnaissance units prior to the attack on Poland cannot be clearly determined. However, on 19 September 1939, immediately after the conclusion of the campaign, the *Oberkommando des Heeres* (OKH – army high command) published a new organizational *Gliederung der Truppen des Heeres* (structure of army forces).

By this time, a further expansion of the *Panzertruppe* had already been decided much earlier. On 1 September 1939, there were five armoured divisions, but to these must be added the four *leichte Divisionen* (leDiv – light [tank] divisions), which, due to being equipped with light tanks and armoured personnel carriers, had a high degree of strategic mobility. Before the outbreak of the war this concept was discarded, and beginning in October the units were converted into regular Panzer divisions: the 1.leDiv became 6.PzDiv; 2.leDiv the 7.PzDiv; 3.leDiv the 8.PzDiv, and the 4.leDiv became the 9.PzDiv.

Guderian and the *Inspektion der Kraftfahrtruppen* (the later *Panzertruppen*) had planned units of battalion strength for modern motorized reconnaissance. The size and equipment of the units were to enable the *Aufklärungs-Abteilung*

Opposite: The German-speaking population cheer elements of an AufklAbt as they enter a town in annexed Bohemia. The motorcycle is followed by a s PzSpWg (8-Rad). Somewhat confusingly, these were designated SdKfz 233 and SdKfz 234 respectively, until 1940, since a large number of PzSpWg (6-Rad) remained in front-line service.

Elements of AufklAbt 3 before the outbreak of war. The luxurious staff car was certainly not covered on battalion level by any organizational structure. The SdKfz 232 (6-Rad) and others of the type were considered to be obsolete before the start of the *Fall Gelb* on 10 May 1940.

(*motorisiert*) to perform a wide variety of tasks. It should be mentioned that before the war some divisions could be issued with two AufklAbt and that reconnaissance elements were also established in regimental strength. The composition of these units also differed greatly depending on the force to which they were attached.

The AufklAbt (mot) of the PzDiv consisted of several companies:

- *Abteilungsstab mit Nachrichtenzug* (staff company with signals platoon)
- *Aufklärungs-Abteilung* (AufklAbt – reconnaissance company)
- *Aufklärungs-Kompanie* (AufklKp – reconnaissance company)
- *Kradschützen-Kompanie* (KradSchtzKp – motorcycle rifle company)
- *schwere Kompanie* (s Kp – heavy company)

In principle, this organization was to remain valid until the end of the war.

Reconnaissance units of varying size and organization were assigned to the various formations in the *Heer* (army).

Army Units (AK Level)

The majority of *Armeekorps* (AK – army corps) existing in 1939, each received a cavalry regiment as a reconnaissance element. But two variations are evident.

The cavalry regiments in II.AK, III.AK, XI.AK and XVII.AK were formed as three battalions consisting of:

- I.*Abteilung: Reiter* (mounted) with three *Reiter-Schwadronen* (mounted squadrons), one MG platoon (horse-drawn) and an anti-tank platoon (both horse-drawn).

- II.*Abteilung: Radfahrer* (bicycle) with three squadrons, a motorized MG squadron and a motorized anti-tank platoon.
- III.*Aufklärungs-Abteilung:* three mounted reconnaissance squadrons, a motorized reconnaissance platoon and a partly motorized signals squadron. The number and type of armoured car is not known.

The I.AK, IV.AK, V.AK, VI.AK, VII.AK, VIII.AK, IX.AK, X.AK, and XII.AK were assigned cavalry regiments with a different structure (two battalions):

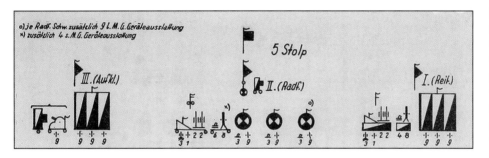

Four reconnaissance regiments, each with three battalions, were formed. The organizational structure for AufklAbt 5 showed a total of only nine armoured reconnaissance vehicles, either Kfz 13 or SdKfz 221, in the two *berittene Abteilungen* (mounted battalions). The third was *Fahrrad-beweglich* (mobile [bicycle]) battalion.

- I.*Aufklärungs-Abteilung* issued with four mounted squadrons, a motorized reconnaissance platoon and a partly motorized signals squadron.
- II.*Radfahrer-Abteilung* with three bicycle squadrons, a motorized MG squadron and a motorized anti-tank platoon.

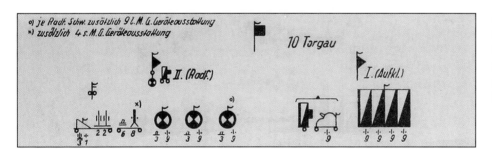

A further nine army corps received reconnaissance regiments, each with a reconnaissance battalion and a bicycle-mounted battalion.

Infantry and Mountain Divisions

The regular infantry and mountain divisions did not have independent reconnaissance detachments. Combat reconnaissance had to be carried out on a case-by-case basis by individual infantry units. Only shortly before the Polish campaign were these units to receive integral reconnaissance detachments. The equipment target consisted of a reconnaissance squadron (mounted), a bicycle squadron and a heavy company/squadron with three 3.7cm *Panzerabwehrkanone* (PaK – anti-tank gun), two 7.5cm *leichte Infanteriegeschütz* (le IG – light infantry guns) 18 as well as two Kfz 13 vehicles or possibly Kfz 14 radio vehicles.

Reconnaissance Elements (InfDiv [mot])

In addition to conventional infantry divisions, which were motorized only to a small extent in 1939, there were tank destroyer elements, signals battalion, machine-gun companies, parts of supply services and engineers. Also, there were four motorized infantry divisions in the field. The latter, because of their greater mobility, also had battalion-sized reconnaissance elements. But again, the allocation was not uniform.

The reconnaissance divisions (mot) of 13.InfDiv, 20.PzDiv, and 29.InfDiv had two *Panzerspäh-Kompanien* (PzSpKp – armoured reconnaissance companies) in addition to the staff section including its signals platoon and two motorcycle rifle platoons.

The 2.InfDiv (mot) had a reconnaissance battalion (AufklAbt 2) similar to the above mentioned, but also a temporary second battalion (AufklAbt 12), which,

Motorized infantry divisions each had one reconnaissance battalion with two reconnaissance companies.

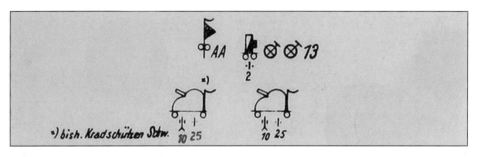

Below: For reasons unknown, 2.InfDiv (mot) was issued a second reconnaissance battalion.

in addition to two PzSpWg was issued with a motorcycle rifle squadron and a heavy platoon (engineers) with three 3.7cm PaK and two 7.5cm le IG 18.

Reconnaissance Elements (leDiv)

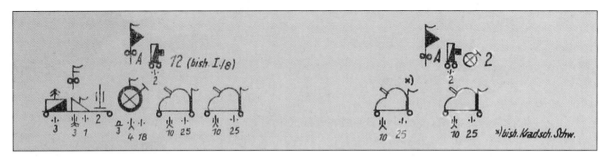

The four light divisions (1.leDiv, 2.leDiv, 3.leDiv and 4.leDiv) available at the beginning of the Polish campaign had, in accordance with their high mobility, very powerful reconnaissance forces from when they were formed. But again, these were organized in an inconsistent manner.

The four light divisions were disbanded after the Polish campaign and re-organized as regular armoured divisions, with corresponding effect on their reconnaissance elements.

Reconnaissance Elements (PzDiv)

The Panzer divisions showed a sufficiently uniform picture with regard to the organization of their reconnaissance elements. By the time of their formation, they corresponded to the above-mentioned basic structure with a staff section, two PzSpWgKp, one KradSchtzKp and one heavy company.

This structure applied to 1.PzDiv, 2.PzDiv, and 5. PzDiv, as well as to 6.PzDiv, 7.PzDiv, 8.PzDiv, and 9.PzDiv, which were formed from the four light divisions. The latter thus had to relinquished their reconnaissance forces during deployment.

For reasons unknown, both 3.Panzer Division and also 4.Panzer Division were each initially issued with two of these reconnaissance battalions in October 1939.

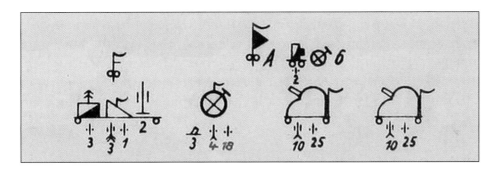

Most PzDiv had the standard organization: one AufklAbt with two PzAufklKp, a KradSchtzKp and a heavy company.

At the time of the publication in October 1939, and thus of course before the start of the Polish campaign, some of these subunits had not yet been fully replenished with equipment.

Below: Reconnaissance elements of 3.PzDiv and 4.PzDiv each had two battalions.

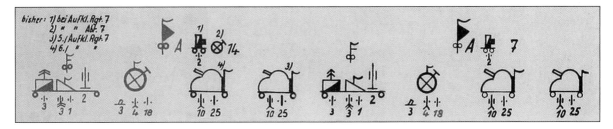

Training Formation

The *Kavallerie-Lehr-Regiment* (cavalry training regiment) garrisoned in Krampnitz/Potsdam served as *Lehr- und Versuchstruppen der Aufklärungstruppe*

The reconnaissance elements of 3.PzDiv and 4.PzDiv each had two battalions.

(training and experimental formation of the reconnaissance troops). This had a Panzer division-type reconnaissance detachment and also a cavalry detachment. Parts of the unit would be deployed for combat in Poland.

Organization

The previously mentioned lack of consistency in the equipping of AufklAbt (mot) probably led to a number of different characteristics, depending on the available material. The most important subunit of the AufklAbt (mot) was the PzSpKp.

Below: Both Kfz 13 and Kfz 14 used the chassis of an Adler 12/55 or a Daimler-Benz 10/50. The open passenger car is a *Gefechtsfahrzeug für Munition und Kraftstoff* (combat car for ammunition and fuel).

The corresponding *Kriegsstärke-Nachweisung* (KStN – table of organizational structure) had been in existence since at least 1935, and KStN 1162 was written specifically for the PzSpKp. These structures were updated at certain intervals according to necessity. (Tragically, none were archived by the units concerned nor at all other command levels, but were destroyed. The majority of those available in present day archives relate to the years 1943 to 1945. Finding earlier tables is purely a matter of luck and

thus rare. This makes it virtually impossible to produce any exact detail of these units before the war.)

When the first reconnaissance battalions were formed in 1935/36, existing vehicles were used. Presumably, the light platoons included a mixture of Kfz 13, MG-armed and Kfz 14 radio vehicles, but also SdKfz 221, SdKfz 222 and SdKfz 223 modern light armoured reconnaissance vehicles when available. The heavy platoons were, where possible, fully equipped with SdKfz 231 and SdKfz 232 (6-Rad) heavy armoured reconnaissance vehicles.

Again, it cannot be stated with any certainty as to whether, in all instances, the required vehicle strengths (five, six or eight armoured vehicles) for the three platoons in a PzSpKp could be met. Mixed equipment certainly occurred, with the more modern vehicles successively replacing the older types: Kfz 13 and Kfz 14 by le PzSpWg and the s PzSpWg (6-Rad) by the s PzSpWg (8-Rad) and also armoured radio cars. Photographs taken during the Polish campaign show that both the Kfz 13 and Kfz 14 and also the PzSpWg (6-Rad) were still in service.

The earliest documented representation of a reconnaissance battalion (mot) was discovered in the files of 6.PzDiv. This very accurate account dates from the formation of the division after it was established from elements of the disbanded 1.leDiv. This unit used only latest type of reconnaissance vehicles.

(Note, some errors were made with the vehicle types when the tables were assmbled. The *Panzerjäger-Zug der schweren Kompanie* [anti-tank platoon of a

Two SdKfz 232 (6-Rad) in service with an AufklAbt (mot) lead a parade through their home garrison town.

Elements of AufklAbt
3 parade near the
Wenceslas Square
in Prague after
the occupation of
Czechoslovakia. At that
time, the reconnaissance
companies were the first
to be equipped with
SdKfz 221. (Getty)

A Kfz 14 *Funkkraftwagen* of AufklAbt 3 (on Daimler-Benz 10/50 chassis). The frame antenna is partly erected.

heavy company] shows a Kfz 60, but this number was never issued. Probably the compiler was referring to a Kfz 69 or Kfz 61.)

Staff Section

The staff consisted of the *Führergruppe* (leader group), the commander of which was issued with an SdKfz 247 Ausf B. His immediate subordinate (deputy), was issued with a Kfz 15 medium cross-country radio car that carries a wide variety of short-range radio equipment. According to the table, this Kfz 15 was assigned to the division staff of 6.PzDiv. The vehicle had a four-man crew which worked in eight-hour shifts to maintain a permanent radio link to the reconnaissance division (mot).

The commander also had five motorcycles at his disposal. Attached to the staff were the combat squadron, the rations squadron, the baggage squadron and the maintenance squadron.

Signals Platoon

An effective signals platoon was attached to the staff of the AufklAbt (mot), an indication of the paramount importance of functioning long-range communications. The *Zugtrupp* (platoon troop) of the signals platoon leader was issued with a Kfz 11, all-terrain vehicle and four motorcycles.

The signals platoon had the following radio equipment:

- Four *mittlerer Funktrupps*, (medium radio squad) 's', each with a Fu 11 radio consisting of a 100W transmitter and a Tornister E 'b'. One SdKfz 263 schwerer Panzerfunkwagen (s PzSpWg – heavy armoured radio vehicle), two Kfz 17, and three unspecified all-terrain vehicles deployed as troop carriers. With a range of 70km (voice) or 200km (Morse), the radios served to connect

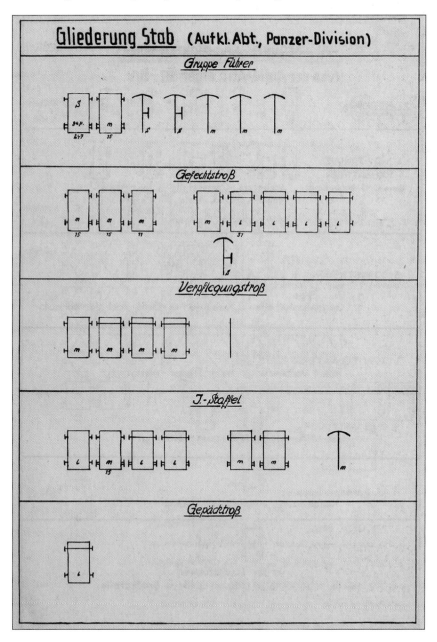

A wartime document dated 1940, showing the organizational structure for the staff of an AufklAbt (mot) in 6.PzDiv.

with the command level of a Panzer division or the command echelons of a battalion and regiment. They also guaranteed permanent communication with the units of the reconnaissance battalion as well as the supporting troops.

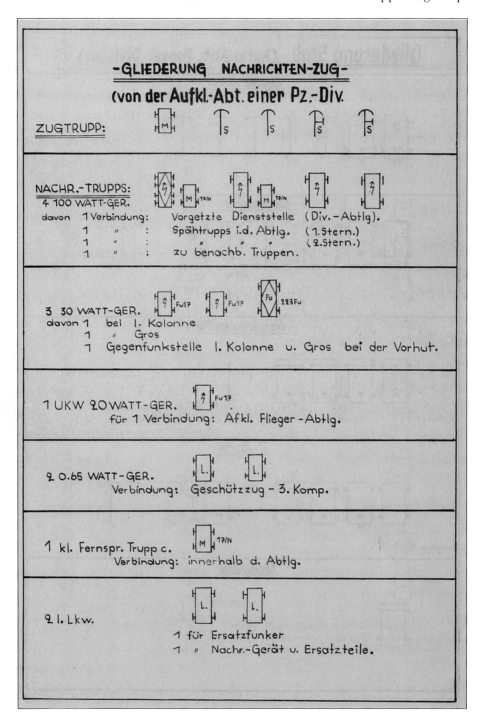

The *Nachrichten-Zug* (NachrZg – signals platoon) of AufklAbt (mot) 6, which in October 1939 was renamed to AufklAbt (mot) 57.

- Three Fu 10, with a range of 40km (voice) to 80km (Morse), were mounted in a SdKfz 223 and two Kfz 17 radio cars. These devices were used for contact with the light column, the main elements of the supply column and also leading reconnaissance elements.
- The FliVO was issued with a Kfz 17 and a Fu 7-equipped *Funktrupp* to maintain contact with *Luftwaffe* crews flying reconnaissance sorties over the battlefront.
- Two Stöwer Kfz 2, light cross-country cars fitted with a portable Tornister Fu 'b1', 'c' or 'f' served as radio vehicles for the gun platoons of 3.*schwere Kompanie* (s Kp – heavy company) within the reconnaissance battalion (mot).
- A small *Fernsprech-Trupp* (telephone squad) was issued with Kfz 17/N to provide and maintain all wire communications within the reconnaissance battalion (mot).

The commander of AufklAbt (mot) 3 was issued with a SdKfz 247 Ausf A. Although a command vehicle, the *schwere geländegängige gepanzerte Kraftwagen* (s gel gep KW – heavy cross-country armoured car), was not equipped with a radio until 1941.

Armoured Car Company

The PzSpKp was the most important element of a reconnaissance battalion (mot) and was structured as follows:

- The *Kompanie-Führer* (company commander) was supplied with an SdKfz 247 Ausf B, armoured command vehicle. His *Kompanie-Truppe* (company command squad) was issued with a cross-country car and a significant number of motorcycles.

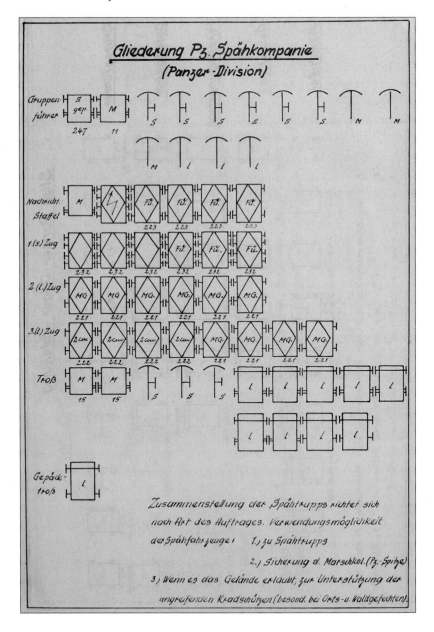

The structure of a PzSpKp, the most important subunit of an AufklAbt.

- The signals squad was issued with four SdKfz 223 and a SdKfz 263 (8-Rad). These had Fu 12, long-range radio equipment and carried an 8m *Kurbelmast*, to facilitate longer range communication.
- The 1.*schwerer Zug* (s Zg – heavy platoon) was issued with an SdKfz 231 (8-Rad) and also an SdKfz 232 (8-Rad).
- The 2.*leichte Zug* (le Zg – light platoon) had six SdKfz 221.
- The 3.*leichte Zug* (light platoon) was issued with four SdKfz 222 and four SdKfz 221.
- The transport column ensured the supply to the PzSpKp.

The composition of the patrols depended on the battlefield situation. The armoured vehicles were assigned to them on a task-by-task basis. Possible duties included:

- Reconnaissance missions on the battlefront.
- Securing the area in front of a marching column of tanks.
- Support attacking motorcycle riflemen, especially when fighting in a town or in woodland.

German troops entering the Sudetenland on 1 October 1938. The leading vehicle, an SdKfz 222 is followed by an SdKfz 223.

Elements of a tank division have been assembled for deployment on the parade ground of their home garrison. Included are a large number of Krupp Kfz 69 artillery tractors towing 3.7cm PaK of the divisional anti-tank battalion and SdKfz 263, most of which were in service with the PzNachrAbt. The Sdkfz 221 were part of the AufklAbt.

Above: In 1939 the PzSpKp attached to 2.PzDiv was issued with all available types of armoured reconnaissance vehicles which included the three types of le PzSpWg then in service as well as 6-Rad and 8-Rad heavy types.

Right: After the occupation of the German-speaking territories in the Sudetenland, Hitler visited, among other places, the town of Eger. The SdKfz 221 is from a unit attached to the *Führerhauptquartier*, Hitler's personal bodyguard.

Motorcycle Company

The *Kradschützen-Kompanie* (KradSchtzKp – motorcycle rifle company) was highly mobile, especially on well-made roads of the western battlefront. The forces were easily deployable and could be used for a wide variety of tasks. A KradSchtzKp was normally issued with more than 50 motorcycles, most of which were *Beiwagen-Kräder* (motorcycle and sidecar [combination]).

Heavy weapons included 18 MG 34 and three 5cm *leichte Granatwerfer* (le GrW – light mortar) 36.

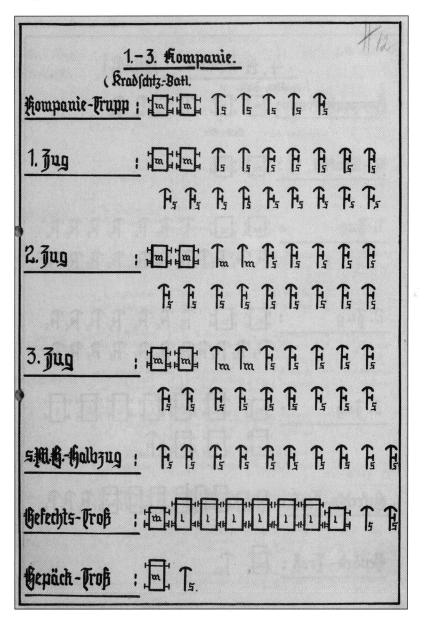

The *Kradschützen-Bataillon* (KradSchtzBtl – motorcycle rifle battalion) was integral part of an AufklAbt (mot).

Heavy Company

The heavy company performed a variety of tasks. As a standardized subunit, it was attached to a number of units, and included engineer forces, anti-tank guns and infantry guns. The engineer platoon was able to create or remove barriers. Furthermore, they deployed large inflatable rafts to to cross waterways obstacles and on many occasions build a temporary light bridge.

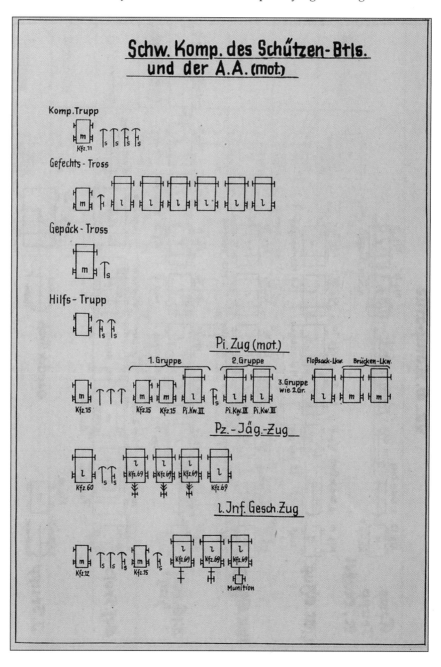

The heavy company of the reconnaissance battalion was equipped with anti-tank and infantry guns.

The tank destroyer platoon was equipped (as of 1938) with three 3.7cm PaK and four Kfz 69, three as towing vehicles and one for use as an ammunition vehicle. The light infantry gun platoon had two 7.5cm le IG 18; Kfz 69s were also available for towing the guns and transporting ammunition. The company had its own supply column, which ensured the delivery of fuel and ammunition as well as rations.

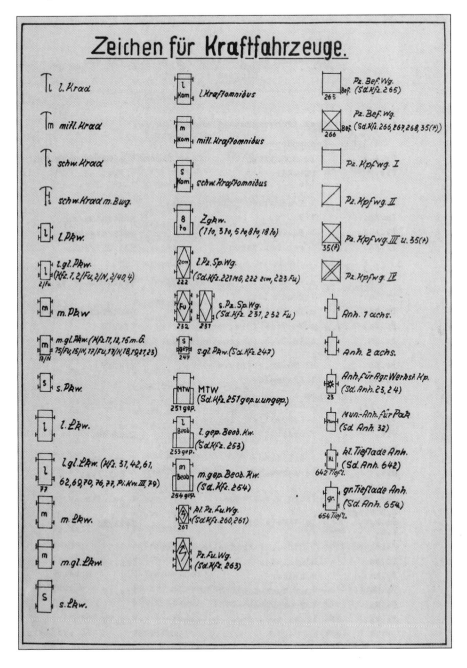

The key to the symbols which indicate the vehicles used in the organizational structures.

The SdKfz 223 (Fu) was wider than the SdKfz 221 to make room for a radio operator. Initially, a Fu 12 transceiver was installed – 80W S, *Empfänger* (Empf – receiver) 'c'. Unlike the SdKfz 260 and SdKfz 261, the type mounted an MG 34 with *Panzerschild* (armoured shield).

Left: A column of vehicles in service with PzAufklAbt 6: an SdKfz 231 (8-Rad) alongside an SdKfz 231 (6-Rad) followed by three un-armed SdKfz 221. The vehicles are in the town of Döberitz, the site of a large training area.

Left: This PzSpWg (6-Rad), followed by an SdKfz 221, is finished in *Buntfarben-Anstrich*, *Reichswehr*-era camouflage. The crew has painted a conspicuous 'F' – *Frisch drauf und durch* (fresh through and through) on their vehicle.

On 1 September 1939, Hitler ordered *Fall Weiss* (Plan White) to commence and German troops sped across the border into Poland. Among those advancing divisions were a number of reconnaissance detachments. After the end of the Polish campaign, experience reports were to be requested from various command levels in all the units involved. The infantry divisions in particular, unanimously complained about the lack of suitable reconnaissance elements.

On 4 October 1939, AufklAbt 161 (61.InfDiv) – the unit was *beritten und Fahrrad beweglich* (mounted on horses and bicycles) – delivered a report:

> The number of radios supplied to the reconnaissance detachment was sufficient. All radio communications worked well with the exception of the 5W radio in the tank reconnaissance unit. Due to the lack of a radio truck, the equipment had to be carried in a passenger car, which did not have suppressed electrics. The TornFu 'b' has proven to be technically reliable, but the weight is still too great, which meant that considerable saddle pressure was unavoidable during a long march or a lengthy scouting operation.
>
> During the execution of reconnaissance along the border between the Reich and Warsaw it became obvious that the often-criticized composition of the reconnaissance detachment (horsemen and cyclists) was, after all, appropriate. As long as firm roads allowed the cyclists to advance without difficulty, they could quickly carry out their ordered reconnaissance. But from Pultusk, deeply rutted paths prevented rapid progress and the marching speed of the cyclists fell below that of the foot soldiers. The horsemen now had to take over the reconnaissance completely. For this purpose, they were supplied with portable radios from stocks held by the detachment.
>
> **General:** The majority of the horses in the mounted squadron were a cross-breed that cannot sustain the required fast marching speed of a cavalry squadron

Opposite: Two Polish officers are being transported on an SdKfz 222, from AufklAbt (mot) 3 (3.PzDiv), back to German-held territory for interrogation.

A SdKfz 233 (8-Rad) and an SdKfz 234 (8-Rad) from AufklAbt (mot) 5 (2.PzDiv). As *Fall Weiss* (Plan White) progressed, Polish gunners began to use the white *Balkenkreuz* as an aiming point. As a result, crews began to paint the marking dark yellow or grey or disguise it with mud.

and, consequently, are not suitable for the required marching performance demanded by the detachment.

The supplementary trucks and cars (*) assigned to the division were not up to the task mechanically; engines and transmissions frequently failed. The shortage of even the smallest spare parts had a particularly detrimental effect. The equipment and performance of the motor-vehicle workshop platoon was extraordinarily poor. There were neither skilled mechanics nor troop engineers available to meet the constant demand for repairs.

(*) These were commercial, basically militarized motor vehicles that performed insufficiently off-road and were also mechanically unreliable.

The report clearly shows the limitations of a conventional infantry division. Apart from the organizational problems, many of the equipment targets proved to be inadequate.

On 5 October 1939, a report was delivered by 217.InfDiv:

Ground Operations: The reconnaissance detachment suffered from the lack of armoured reconnaissance vehicles that could have provided support for the bicycle-mounted scouting parties. The commandeered civilian cars proved unsuitable for the sandy roads in Poland; they frequently broke down and were abandoned in the field. Also, light vehicles were completely useless for towing anti-tank and light infantry guns.

Shortly before the invasion of Poland, large numbers of commercially available vehicles were confiscated by the military from German companies and private individuals to be delivered to the army, another indication of the insufficient capacity in industrial production. These civilian vehicles did not meet the requirements of the military at all and proved to be unreliable. Classified as *Personenkraftwagen* (o) (Pkw – personnel carrier) and *Lastkraftwagen* (o) (Lkw – truck), where (o) indicates civilian origin, these partly militarized passenger cars and trucks were not very popular because they were too lightly built and did not all-wheel drive. Whereas, those specialized off-road vehicles developed before the war performed well:

The Stöwer-built Kfz 2/2 radio car, was the only vehicle that could follow the reconnaissance regiment over any terrain.

The Kfz 15 should completely replace the older Kfz 12. Importantly, all motor vehicles for use in the East must have four-wheel drive.

A mixed reconnaissance unit of AufklAbt (mot) 3 enters a Polish village. The crews have used mud to disguise the conspicuous white crosses on their vehicles.

Elements of the AufklAbt in 2.leDiv are being supplied in a wooded area. A *Feldküche* (field kitchen) has been established ready to supply hot food. The all-wheel-drive *Einheitsdiesel* (standardized diesel) trucks had a remarkable off-road capability, but proved to be mechanically too complex for military use.

Motorcycles, with the exception of the light type, have had only limited success and would have to be kept to the minimum for cavalry units.

On 17 October 1939, 11.InfDiv reported:

Land operations: Inadequate reconnaissance resulted immediately in many avoidable casualties. The lack of suitable maps has had a detrimental effect on the deployment of reconnaissance troops.

The above is not surprising, since the reconnaissance elements in a standard infantry division were not sufficiently equipped or trained for a *Blitzkrieg* (lightning war). Probably part of the problem lay in the lack of training exercises combined with other factors. It would be a long time before German infantry units became fully motorized.

On 29 September 1939, the XIX.*Armeekorps* sent a report to *Heeresgruppe Nord* (Army Group North) with a copy for the *Oberbefehlshaber des Heeres* (ObdH – commander-in-chief of the army). Guderian now had four major units at his disposal for the invasion of Poland:

- The 3.PzDiv (two tank regiments).
- PzDiv Kempf (a PzRgt) – recently formed in annexed Bohemia.

- 2.InfDiv (mot).
- 20.InfDiv (mot).

All four divisions were fully motorized as required by Guderian for his vision of highly mobile warfare. The equipment of the reconnaissance elements of the armoured divisions was described as basically sufficient as long as they were integrated in action. If they were, then all required tasks could be fully accomplished.

Guderian, however, saw a major problem in the fact that during operations all command levels of the armoured divisions (tank brigade, regiment, and division) constantly requested reinforcement from the troops of AufklAbt (mot). These requests were often granted by the division command.

The fragmentation of the forces of the reconnaissance division threatened to weaken them unduly. This meant that, during an attack, a mission was often compromised. As a result, Guderian, who since 1938 had also been *Chef der Schnellen Truppen* (chief of the rapid forces), demanded the creation of separate close-range and combat reconnaissance elements for the Panzer-Brigade and also the *Schützen-Brigade* in Panzer divisions. Since each of these already had a light armoured platoon, Guderian called for appropriate reconnaissance tanks to be delivered. He was referring to the 'PzKpfw II with fast tracks': this was the PzKpfw II Ausf D, which was in service with the highly mobile light divisions. Guderian even expressed his requirements for improvements. For example, he demanded improved vision devices including the fitting of an (armoured) observation dome for the commander or the installation of more observation periscopes. For the infantry divisions (mot), he demanded that the number of reconnaissance elements be increased to the same level as those AufklAbt (mot) in Panzer divisions.

Guderian found words of praise for the deployment of the various reconnaissance units, but at the same time called for more responsibility when planning combat missions. In his experience, any haphazard use of the divisions, or deployment at night, frequently led to heavy, avoidable losses. His demands also represented his maximum requirements, but they could not be met immediately.

This is confirmed in a letter from the OKH, dated 27 October 1939:

Requirements that are recognized as legitimate, cannot currently be met in the numbers requested, for following reasons:

1.) Tanks: Deployment of the four companies is not possible for due to the lack of equipment. Procurement of the PzKpfw IV will be accelerated as far as possible.

2.) Armoured reconnaissance and motor vehicles: Equipping the armoured and rifle brigades, rifle regiments, and infantry regiments (mot) with armoured scout cars, as well as equipping them with the other armoured motor vehicles required for various units, is not possible in the foreseeable future.

3.) Artillery: Reinforcement of the light artillery division in a PzDiv cannot be accomplished. Any equipping with anti-tank rifles will not be possible for several months.

The four-man crew of a s PzSpWg (8-Rad) had five hatches from which to exit the vehicle in case of emergency.

The 2.leDiv was also involved in the Polish campaign as a highly mobile armoured unit. In a field report, dated 8 October 1939, the commander writes of the experiences faced by AufklRgt 7. (In contrast to the Panzer divisions, the light divisions received regimental-sized reconnaissance elements, presumably in view of their much greater tactical range):

Many reconnaissance units used the initial letter of a city to identify an individual vehicles. Dresden indicates this is vehicle 'D'.

In many instances, reconnaissance over large areas never produced results. Even when a large number of vehicles were deployed for the reconnaissance of multiple objectives, success was not guaranteed even when supported by combat forces. As a result, large numbers of reconnaissance vehicles were lost.

The best vehicle was still the SdKfz 231 (8-Rad), since all other types were not capable of off-road driving and also frequently broke down, often in the middle of enemy lines or in their field of fire.

The MG-armed Kfz 13 must be described as unsuitable, since both the armour and armament are inadequate.

The organization of reconnaissance, combined with an AufklRgt, has not proved

successful. The regiment is too strong for reconnaissance and too weak for combat.

For a light division, a reconnaissance detachment of two *Panzerspäh-Schwadronen* (PzSpSchw – armoured reconnaissance squadrons) each with 25 vehicles and a KradSchtzKp is sufficient.

We propose the introduction of a standard vehicle capable of running on tracks or, whenever necessary, on wheels. It would be desirable for the type to mount a 3.7cm gun and also a heavy machine gun.

The mission of this unit is close tactical and combat reconnaissance. Long-range tactical reconnaissance, which the light division absolutely needs, is the responsibility of the *Heeresflieger-Staffel* [army aviation unit] operated by the *Luftwaffe* attached to the division. It rendered excellent service to the division during the advance towards the river Vistula.

As the fighting progressed, the division disbanded the reconnaissance regiment and established a reconnaissance leader at the division staff. This procedure proved successful. The division commander organizes the operation, while the reconnaissance commander orders the forces necessary and provides a ready reserve of scouts. The KradSchtz battalion was placed under the immediate command of the division for combat operations.

Current value of the combat troops

The value of the unit is limited by the losses, especially of experienced officers, but it has gained more valuable battlefield experience. The loss of vehicles, and especially of those for reconnaissance, is not sufficient as to have decisive impact on combat operations. For the restoration of full operational readiness, as at the beginning of the war, priority must be given to training the replacement of officers, NCOs, and *Mannschaften* [enlisted men] and also the thorough overhaul of vehicles. For this purpose, the supply of spare parts and the establishment of efficient workshop facilities is vital and must equal those at our home bases.

The note from the commander regarding his experience is understandable. It is interesting to observe that in no case could long-range reconnaissance be carried out successfully. The objection is justified, since the AufklRgt was only partially capable of such missions. Deployed over a wide area, without a link to the Panzer division, it lacked rear cover and, should it be needed, support from combat fighting tanks. The losses referred to were possibly due to a lack of combat experience on the part of the commander and his troops and the consequent mistaken deployment of light armoured vehicles.

When 2.leDiv went into combat with a reconnaissance regiment, at least the AufklAbt (mot) 12 corresponded exactly to the structure required by the commander. The two armoured reconnaissance squadrons of the second

Opposite: Although the frame-type antenna fitted on all production s PzSpWg (6-Rad) (Fu) was conspicuous, it continued to be used on the later s PzSpWg (8-Rad). It was not until 1942 that it was replaced by the *Sternantenne* 'd'. The rear door could only be opened when the spare wheel was folded down.

The crew of an SdKfz 232 (8-Rad), from an unknown AufklAbt (mot), observe a group of German field engineers as they remove anti-tank obstacles positioned on the Polish border.

AufklAbt (mot) most certainly represented a valuable reinforcement, but they had to be used responsibly.

The mechanical problems, on the other hand, are understandable. The unit was partly equipped with Kfz 13 and Kfz 14, which were not up to the demands of modern warfare.

The commander further points out problems with the NachtAbt, which did not meet his requirements in terms of numbers and equipment. The hint at switching to wired (telephone) communication as a consequence of these problems seems unacceptable for a tank division. The reconnaissance division in particular needs functioning and reliable radio communications. The basic concept of 2.leDiv was not successful: after the Polish campaign, the unit was disbanded, and PzAbt 66 was to be assigned to the newly formed 7.PzDiv in 1940. Half of AufklRgt 7 was used to create KradSchtzBtl 7 while the rest of the regiment remained attached to 7.PzDiv.

After the end of the Polish campaign the commander of 1.PzDiv delivered a report, dated 23 January 1940, in which he concurred with Guderian. In order to relieve pressure on his AufklAbt, he requested all subunits of the division to conduct independent reconnaissance.

It was vital to conceal reconnaissance vehicles. Here an s PzSpWg (8-Rad) has been positioned between two stacks of cut hay while engineers carry out routine maintenance.

Approach and execution of reconnaissance, and the training of units

During the campaign in Poland and during all training exercises I have the perceived that reconnaissance of any kind (long-range, close-range and combat, as well as air reconnaissance) was very often wrongly ordered and executed, and often completely omitted.

For these reasons, reconnaissance often failed, resulting in high casualties. The failure of reconnaissance led to unpleasant surprises for the troops when advancing on the enemy. I propose that in the future, all reconnaissance should be carried out with regard to the following points:

a.) Effective reconnaissance results in the best security.

b.) Every unit must systematically conduct close-range and combat reconnaissance and report observations.

c.) Combat and close reconnaissance also includes aerial operations, which must be conducted before (and during) every march or before it halts.

d.) Each scouting party must be briefed on the general situation.

e.) If a clash with the enemy is probable, then a step-by-step approach – rather than rapid terrain gain – is preferred.

f.) A group approach on roads and tracks is wrong. The patrols must drive with large safety distances, and any stop must be made behind cover. The rest of the approach is carried out progressively and supported by covering fire from other units in the patrol. The approach to a town, village or woodland, must always be carried out in widely dispersed formation.

g.) The patrol should only observe and report. It fights only when necessary to fulfill the combat mission.

h.) Tank patrols must be off the road, avoiding any towns or woodland.

i.) Only special circumstances may require a different procedure. In addition, the AufklAbt is responsible for the training of the *Spähtrupps* [reconnaissance teams] of other subunits. I request the commanders to accelerate this training with all vigor. The present situation is not yet satisfactory.

I will visit these reconnaissance detachments in the first half of February and review their skills in this regard.

The first *Waffen*-SS units were also deployed during the Polish campaign, but under the command of the *Oberkommando der Wehrmacht* (OKW – high command of the defence forces).

After Hitler seized power, the SS-*Verfügungstruppe* was officially established in parallel to the *Sturmabteilung* (SA) as an auxiliary police force. In 1933, SS-*Division Leibstandarte* Adolf Hitler (LAH) was established and this was followed by the first internal political trial of strength which saw the old SA finally disempowered. The SS formations then became the *Partei-Armee* (army

Although the infantry divisions relied on horse-drawn transport many also had armoured reconnaissance forces. Here a supply column is passed by an early production SdKfz 223. Note, the vehicle is armed with a 7.92mm MG 13 and has which has simple plate steel covers over the vision apertures. (Getty)

of the NSDAP) and its armed units began to operate in the same way as the *Wehrmacht* troops. The leaders and troops were sworn to be loyal to Adolf Hitler and uphold the ideology of the NSDAP.

Where the *Wehrmacht* traditionally saw itself as an executive organ of the government, and thus as apolitical, the NSDAP planned, in the long-term, to replace it with a political army. Although Hitler had often assured *Wehrmacht* officials that it would remain the nation's sole weapons carrier, unease about the emerging *Waffen*-SS spread throughout all levels of command.

In 1939, SS units as a whole represented only a small percentage of the total troop strength. During the Polish campaign, several SS-*Standarten* (regiments) were attached to PzDiv Kempf:

SS-*Standarte Deutschland*
SS-*Artillerie-Regiment*
SS-*Aufklärungs-Abteilung*
SS-*Nachrichten-Abteilung*
SS-*Flamm-Maschinengewehr-Kompanie*

The *Armeeoberkommando* (AOK – army high command) 3, to which the PzDiv Kempf was attached, prepared a report after the end of the campaign. It was delivered to the commander of *Heeresgruppe Nord* (Army Group North):

> The level of training and leadership of the SS units showed many deficiencies which caused serious friction with other [German] troops that frequently led to altercations during the battles. Their dedication to fighting and their particularly good equipment failed to compensate for these deficiencies. The reports from the *Führungsstab* (command staff) and PzDiv Kempf are incorporated.

The report from the *Führungsstab* was devastating:

Report on the combat value of the SS units attached to PzDiv Kempf

The SS-AufklAbt (two KradSchtzKp) did not fulfill any of its tasks. It was unable to penetrate even minimal enemy opposition. Even when only weak enemy resistance was expected or when reconnaissance was conducted from a long way away, no usable reconnaissance results were obtained. On several occasions, the failure of the SS-AufklAbt placed our commanders and troops in an often precarious position. Whether a lack of training or a lack of acumen was the reason for this failure is difficult to judge.

In the corps area, the SS units were among the only units that, on several occasions, retreated from an enemy attack.

A high-ranking officer in a Mercedes staff car, passes a column of armoured reconnaissance vehicles after the successful conclusion of the Polish campaign. (Getty)

Although in some cases this action was tactically prudent, bravado hindered performance. Worryingly, the attitude of the SS units toward the civilian population, in the rear area, was in contradiction to the principles that should be observed at all times by the German soldier.

The lack of discipline was particularly conspicuous during marches. It was also noted that SS leaders and their subordinates disprespected army officers, which was coupled with an over-confident assessment of their combat performance.

The assessments of the same SS units written by the adjutant of PzDiv Kempf, is diametrically opposite to that of the *Führungsstab*:

3.SS-AufklAbt

Led by its exceptionally enthusiastic and enterprising commander, SS-*Sturmbann-Führer* Brandt, the battalion performed excellently in reconnaissance, attack and defence. These achievements are especially commendable since the battalion had only four armoured reconnaissance vehicles and therefore had to perform difficult reconnaissance tasks with its two KradSchtz companies. Brandt is the type of person who gets difficulties out of the way and approaches every task with passion. Every man is sworn to uphold special vows.

The significant discrepancies between these assessments suggest that the truth lay somewhere in the middle.

Before the campaign, many infantry divisions were assigned reconnaissance detachments, but these later had to be relinquished. This practice led to corresponding claims. For example, on 13 October 1939, when the division was fighting as part of the XIX.AK and was advancing from the German eastern border eastward through the so-called 'Polish Corridor', which connected Poland to the Baltic Sea, the commander of 23.InfDiv wrote:

Ground Reconnaissance

The view that the reconnaissance detachment should not be given combat missions was proven wrong during fighting in the corridor. In almost every engagement, the AufklAbt was involved in battles, usually of extended duration, in which it had to defend the terrain it had just won. This will always happen on its own, with or without orders. Therefore, the AufklAbt of an infantry division must have the firepower to cover all necessities. The attached AufklAbt should remain permanently assigned to the infantry division even in peacetime.

The available AufklAbt has three speeds (bicycle, horse or motor). This complicates command and destroys the unity of the AufklAbt. The existing armoured reconnaissance vehicles (Kfz 13) have proved useless.

The quality of the armament was basically described as somewhere between sufficient and good in all reports. Especially, the MG 34 was highly appreciated because it had a high rate of fire. Although the weapon was susceptible to dust, careful cleaning by the crew kept it in firing condition. The importance of heavy weapons (3.7cm PaK and 7.5cm infantry guns) continued to be emphasized.

Before the launch of *Fall Weiss*, there were no dedicated training instructions for the tactical use of the reconnaissance units. As a result, *Kavallerie-Lehr-Regiment*, garrisoned at Krampnitz Kaserne, near Potsdam in 1937, was tasked with developing exercises for deployment and battlefield tactics. Elements from this unit were part of the force deployed for the invasion of Poland.

This s PzSpWg (8-Rad) has received a heavy hit which has torn the 14.5mm thick armour apart and completely destroyed the interior.

5

After the conclusion of the Polish campaign, the experience of the units involved was evaluated in a wide variety of areas (organization, equipment and tactics).

At the beginning of 1940, preparations were already underway for the next military campaign, the invasion of Western Europe. In May 1940, a total of ten Panzer divisions were available, and the number of InfDiv and InfDiv (mot) had also been increased.

The OKH periodically produced an overview of the division of the field army. Many of these are still available and the January and April 1940 issues provide information on how reconnaissance units were equipped.

With one exception, reconnaissance units were no longer available at the army troop level, but were directly attached to other units.

Infantry Divisions

The standard infantry divisions still had very different reconnaissance elements. Certainly, not all could be assigned a AufklAbt, some received only a reconnaissance squadron, others were assigned only platoon-size reconnaissance elements.

Some of the InfDiv of the first and second waves were issued with reconnaissance detachments consisting of a mounted squadron, a bicycle squadron, and a mixed heavy squadron which, in addition to 3.7cm PaK and 7.5cm le IG 18, also had three light armoured scout cars. A not insignificant portion of the InfDiv deployed in these waves was equipped with reconnaissance elements the size of single bicycle squadron.

All the infantry divisions of the third wave (formed in the September of 1939) were similarly differently equipped. One part had only a bicycle

Opposite: A total of ten SdKfz 247 Ausf A were built on the six-wheel chassis of a Krupp Kfz 69. The vehicle was not equipped with radios and was lightly armoured against standard infantry ammunition and shrapnel. The divisional symbol (partly obliterated) for 7.PzDiv and the tactical sign for a AufklKp are painted on the rear. The large Nazi flag was used to identify the vehcle as 'friendly' to *Luftwaffe* pilots.

Both reconnaissance and intelligence divisions were issued with the SdKfz 263 PzFuWg. These vehicles are in service with NachrAbt 90 (10.PzDiv). The barely visible 'K', next to the tactical sign, indicates that the vehicle is in service with *Panzergruppe* (tank group) von Kleist. Each carry a *Fascine* (bundle of sticks) for crossing soft ground or a shallow ditch.

squadron and an anti-tank platoon. Other units were equipped with an independent platoon issued with three light armoured scout cars. In fact, this corresponded to the equipment of the basically better equipped InfDiv of the first and second waves.

The InfDiv of the fourth wave (also formed in September 1939) were equipped with *Radfahrer* squadrons as well as motorized anti-tank platoons.

The reconnaissance units (the use of *Abteilung* [battalion] was explicitly avoided, with *Einheit* [unit] being the norm) of the infantry divisions of the fifth wave (September 1939) as well as of the sixth wave (November 1939) even had only one bicycle squadron with nine machine guns.

In the InfDiv of the seventh wave, the reconnaissance elements (one bicycle squadron) were merged with the divisional tank destroyer company.

Infantry Divisions (mot)

The equipment of the motorized (2.InfDiv, 13.InfDiv, 16.InfDiv, 20.InfDiv, 29.InfDiv, and 60.InfDiv was standardized, and all had virtually identical reconnaissance detachments before the French campaign, with one motorcycle infantry squadron and one armoured reconnaissance squadron. There was no heavy squadron with anti-tank or infantry guns.

Mountain Divisions

Like the normal infantry divisions, the 1.*Gebirgsdivision* (GebDiv – mountain division), 2.GebDiv and 3.GebDiv were equipped only with mounted reconnaissance elements as well as KradSchtz.

Panzer Divisions

Nine of the ten Panzer divisions were equipped with an AufklAbt. These had the familiar basic structure:

- Staff
- Two armoured reconnaissance companies
- One KradSchtz squadron
- One heavy squadron

Conversely, 9.PzDiv, which had been formed in January 1940 from the former 4.leDiv, had a strong reconnaissance regiment (mot). In addition to the standard equipment mentioned above, the division had at its disposal two additional KradSchtz squadrons and as well as a larger number of infantry guns and *Granatwerfer* (GrW – mortars). After the end of the French campaign,

The 2cm KwK 30 L/55 and MG 34, as well as the *Turm-Zielfernrohr* (TZF – turret sighting telescope) 3a and the *Fliegervisier* (anti-aircraft mounting) 38, were mounted coaxially.

the AufklAbt (mot) in all Panzer divisions had only one PzSpKp. However, it is possible that these units were needed to equip the newly created Panzer divisions during the 'miraculous proliferation' at the turn of 1940/41, further evidence of the lack of heavy industry in Germany.

Waffen-SS Units

While the SS-*Verfügungs-Division* (also called *Leibstandarte* SS-Adolf Hitler) had a weak reconnaissance detachment with a sole PzSpKp, the newly raised SS-*Division Totenkopf* had only two KradSchtzAbt. In August 1940, these reconnaissance elements were reinforced with a platoon of armoured scout cars.

Panzer-Aufklärungs-Lehr-Abteilung

During the French campaign, only one reconnaissance unit was deployed at army troop level. This unit, the *Panzer-Aufklärungs-Lehr-Abteilung* (PzAufklLehrAbt – armoured reconnaissance training battalion), produced an extensive field report after the successful completion of the invasion.

A reconnaissance squad from AufklAbt 90 (10. PzDiv) in a French village. The composition of a squad depended on their mission, the minimum being two cars of which one had to be a radio vehicle, here an SdKfz 232.

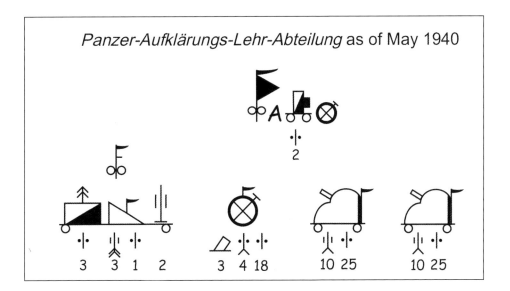

Panzer-Aufklärungs-Lehr-Abteilung as of May 1940

The PzAufklLehrAbt (here the term *Panzer-Aufklärung* is used for the first time) corresponded in structure to a large or reinforced reconnaissance division (mot).

Field report on the operations from 9 May to 30 June 1940.

Combat Value: The training of the battalion was at a high level. The experiences of the campaign in Poland could be fully evaluated during the long training period in the Rhineland. Likewise, it had been possible to bring the armoured reconnaissance squadron, newly assigned to the AufklAbt at the beginning of 1940, whose training condition at first left considerable to be desired, fully in line with the other squadrons.

Ongoing Trials: During the mission, the following equipment was still being tested:
• *Bord-zu-Bord* equipment (*) in all armoured vehicles.
• *Flieger-Notvisier* (emergency anti-aircraft sight) for 2cm FlaK 30 in all light PzSpWg (2cm).

Opponent: The Belgian practically did not appear as an opponent. The French fought bravely at first, but after reaching the Somme, the will to fight diminished considerably. After crossing the Orne River, hardly any French troops fought, with the exception of navy fusiliers and their colonial troops. The latter put up much tougher resistance than other French troops. The British fought valiantly and decently everywhere until the surrender.

Opposing materiel: The French often used older but fully capable equipment. The battalion encountered many armoured scout cars, but relatively few tanks. The British, in turn, used many light and medium tanks but few armoured scout cars.

The well-maintained
road surfaces in the
Low Countries and
France allowed German
reconnaissance forces to
rapidly redeploy, which
helped armoured and
infantry units maintain
the *Blitzkrieg*. (Getty)

This s PzSpWg (Fu) (8-Rad) early production still has the frame for carrying the command authority symbol and a pivoting arm-type antiaircraft bracket; both were soon to be dropped. Note, 15l triangular-shaped fuel canisters stowed next to the driving lamps. The tools on the front plate were standard German issue.

Deployment: The division saw action in Luxembourg, Belgium and France. Initially it fought as an army unit with *Heeresgruppe* A. The units were mostly deployed on the flanks. These missions were fully in line with the capabilities of the battalion, the disadvantages of the constantly changing attachments, especially in the supply forces, were accepted.

Casualties: The battalion lost one officer, two NCOs, and 18 enlisted men. Five heavy PzSpWg and two light PzSpWg were lost, most to enemy fire.

Tactical Deployment: The first patrol wave, especially on the route of our advance, must have a lead of at least one hour – if possible two. The AufklAbt must not chase the leading patrols. Security on the march is provided by an orderly column and by security intervals. There is no more than five minutes between the vanguard and the bulk of the division. The scouting party in front is placed under the command of the leader of the advance guard; if possible, it should be from the same squadron.

The assignment of elements in the tank destroyer platoon has proved expedient. If armoured enemy appears, the anti-tank guns are immediately on the spot and do not have to be laboriously pulled forward past the division. Despite all misgivings about keeping the PzSpWg squadrons apart, it proved necessary during the advance to assign some light armoured scout cars to the unarmoured sections as protection against snipers or attacks from the flanks or rear.

The gun platoon [7.5cm le IG 18] is best placed in the main body of the battalion, since from there it can more easily find a suitable firing position. If it travels in the vanguard, combat distances of no more than 800m result, which does not correspond to the most favourable firing range of 1,500m to 1,800m.

When crossing wide roads, the temporary establishment of lateral safety barriers has proven to be very expedient. These may have to be set up separately for the vanguard and the main body. The main body must provide flank protection from its own units, since otherwise the elements assigned to the advance guard will not be able to join up with them, or will do so too late. Thus, when the enemy is very close, the division travels in an *'Igel'* [hedgehog] staggered formation.

The division commander must be well forward with his command vehicle in order to lead effectively. At every halt, it is imperative to remain spaced and get under cover against enemy aircraft.

The *Igel* formation has also proven very effective for securing surprise targets and at assembly areas and resting points. The securing itself is done by PaK, KradSchtz and *Pioniere* [field engineers]. An allocation of armoured reconnaissance vehicles will be the exception. The forces available to the AufklAbt are sufficient only for its own protection. The use of scout cars as armoured lead vehicles for other units is already prohibited according to army orders.

This *gemischte Spähtrupp* (mixed patrol) is led by a s PzSpWg (8-Rad), followed by two PzSpWg (6-Rad). Note, the two smoke grenades fitted, as a temporary expedient, on the front plate of the leading vehicle.

Above: 19 March 1940: *Wehrmacht Tag* (Armed Forces Day) on 18 and 19 March 1940. An s PzSpWg (8-Rad) being demonstrated to the public. The type could easily cross a 1.8m-wide ditch, climb over a 50cm high obstacle and negotiate water 100cm deep.

Right: This s PzSpWg (6-Rad) has received a direct hit by a high-explosive shell which has torn apart the 8mm side armour and mortally wounded the crew.

Reconnaissance: For armoured reconnaissance squads, the requirement must be that they are equipped with at least one, preferably two, 2cm KwK 38 L/55 guns. The question of the further comptosition of the reconnaissance troops depends on the availability of armoured vehicles. For patrols with long-range objectives, the battalion prefers the heavy (possibly reinforced) patrol, since the lead vehicle (8-Rad) can retreat quickly, thanks to its reverse driver, in the event of a sudden appearance of anti-tank fire. What is necessary, however, is the introduction of an effective sighting device in the turret roof and a serviceable BzB radio (*) for all, and a smoke grenade discharger that can be operated from inside the vehicle. Furthermore, the following compositions have proven to be ideal for patrols:

• Lead vehicle: SdKfz 231 or SdKfz 222
• Reconnaisance squad leader: SdKfz 232 or SdKfz 223
• Third vehicle: SdKfz 221

The advantages of the SdKfz 222 as a lead vehicle compared to the SdKfz 231 are its better field of view to all sides (open turret). Both target acquisition and observation of the firing results, by the commander, are significantly better. Furthermore, the SdKfz 222 presents a smaller target. However, the introduction of a closed turret and a second (reversing) driver is desirable (**).

Reconnaissance squads without 2cm KwK 30 L/55 cannot be used for important missions, as fighting develops during almost all operations. The effect of the 2cm KwK 30 gun has often proved decisive. Scouting parties without this weapon can only be, at most, used for establishing contact.

For the actual reconnaissance activity, the existing principles have certainly proven to be effective.

The AufklAbt (mot) cannot operate at night with its present equipment (exception: a moonlit night). After dark, therefore, scouting parties can only be deployed for a very urgent mission and then only on foot. In this way, no clear evidence of enemy positions can be obtained.

During reconnaissance, an attack by anti-tank weapons must always be expected. The fighting on the Somme has shown that approaching to within range of enemy anti-tank weapons usually resulted in the loss of the vehicle. Furthermore, once the enemy becomes alerted, further reconnaissance will be considerably hampered, if not prevented. For aggressive reconnaissance against weak enemy forces, the assignment of motorcycle gunners or sappers to the reconnaissance force is necessary and expedient. After overcoming the first resistance, however, the reconnaissance parties must continue to advance for further without these reinforcements, the inclusion of non-armoured elements would only hinder the reconnaissance party. Armoured protection for these reinforcements therefore seems desirable and could be achieved by converting the KradSchtz squadron into one equipped with armoured vehicles. [***]

Kradschützen-Spähtrupps [motorcycle reconnaisance squads]

The allocation of two machine guns for mobile patrols proved advantageous. Mounted on the first two sidecars ready to fire, they could provide protection for each other in an emergency. Unfortunately, carrying *Tornister-Funkgeräte* (TornFu – portable radios) in a motorcycle sidecar was usually futile, since the distances were almost always too great. If a SdKfz 223 was assigned as a radio car, the high cross-country mobility KradSchtz reconnaissance squad would be significantly compromised

Combat

Superiority when scouting in the reconnaissance area is achieved only by rapidly attacking the enemy observation units. For the most part, however, the battalion received other combat missions, such as holding narrow areas of open terrain or taking possession of crossings. Despite regulations, the firepower of the battalion was not reinforced and this made it impossible for the force to perform additional tasks. For battalion-strength combat, the existing principles have proven correct. The KradSchtz actually lead the fight, but alone the *Kradschützen* squadron is too weak, in the best case it has (without heavy MG and light mortars) only 54 fighters. The question of a fundamental reinforcement of the combat power of the AufklAbt (mot) requires further consideration.

To support and reinforce the KradSchtz squadron, the division established a light motorcycle reconnaissance platoon, which primarily supported the vanguard in quickly breaking weak resistance. This platoon had a strength of two off-road passenger cars, two Kfz 18 combat vehicles, two solo motorcycles, and 16 heavy motorcycles with a sidecars. This platoon could be established only by the division commander somewhat recklessly taking personnel and equipment from not only by the light column but also other combat squadrons.

The light platoon was an absolute success and was used during marches without coming into contact with the enemy to cordon off roads, for relaying messages and other tasks. When advancing it would quickly occupy and hold points important to the division, where it would drive away enemy scouting parties, break light enemy resistance, support the KradSchtz Squadron and provide local security. Often the platoon formed a most welcome reserve in the hands of the battalion commander, especially when the KradSchtz squadron was in combat. For dedicated securing duties, the two half-platoons were equipped with additional machine guns captured from enemy forces. The *Panzerbüchse* (PzB – anti-tank rifle) was often successfully used to secure an objective.

These principles must also be taken into account in the fast-moving combat operations of an AufklAbt (mot).

The use of light flamethrowers, which unfortunately were not available to the battalion, appears to be particularly useful and promising for fighting against pillboxes and for the frequently required local combat.

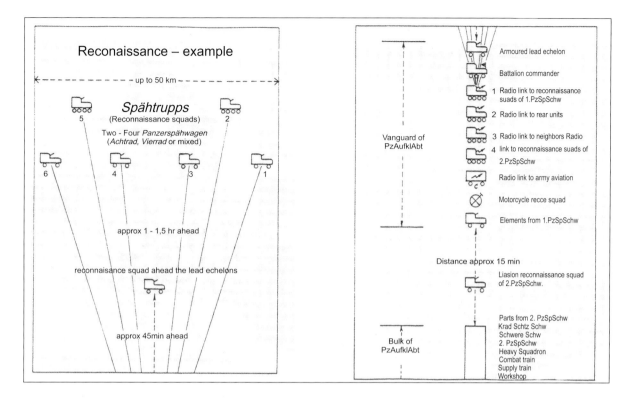

The 2cm KwK 30 L/55 has proved to be a weapon that has a special effect on the moral of enemy troops. Its use in combat should be accelerated.

Radio Communications

The radio sections of the signals platoon had fully proved their worth during the operation. Command of the detachment by radio was assured at all times. Certain difficulties were encountered; however, this was due to the different frequency ranges of the old and new 30W transmitters. The lack of range of the 30W transmitter compared to the 100W type was disadvantageous for patrol missions over distances of more than 80km. Both disadvantages would disappear with the introduction of a standard transmitter for all AufklAbt (mot).

The number of available radio stations of an AufklAbt (mot) is just sufficient in full operation, but it was not possible to hold reserves. The remote stations of the light reconnaissance units were manned by four reconnaissance squads each in full operation. Two of the 30W devices [Fu 10] had to be reserved for liaison with the main part of the battalion and also the signals squadron. The two remaining 30W devices are used by four scout squads and quickly become overburdened making the rapid transmission of messages impossible under all circumstances. Therefore, consideration should be given to assigning a fifth 30W radio squad to the division. For this the two portable radios could be dropped. The range of

These diagrams, taken from an original document, show the prescribed structure of the PzAufklAbt in combat and on the march.

A 6.PzDiv forward observation post concealed in a wheat field, as German forces advance into France. Two *Kradmelder* (dispatch riders) stand ready to deliver information to other parts of the division. (Getty)

An s PzSpWg (Fu) (8-Rad), from AufklAbt 5 (2.PzDiv), has suffered a mechanical failure. Engineers have removed all the weapons while they wait for a recovery vehicle to arrive.

these radios is too short for an AufklAbt, and it is practically impossible for any communications to be sent while on the move. At night, the equipment is seriously affected by atmospheric interference.

The 20W *Fliegergerät* (Fu 7) performed very well. Unfortunately, there was no opportunity to trial it for ground-to-air communication. Consequently, experience with the transmitter is not available. For tactical reasons, however, such radio traffic would be very desirable, since listening to *Luftwaffe* reconnaissance aircraft would be an extremely important source of information. Tests between the our FliVO and aircraft flying near our position, and also the AufklAbt (mot) would have determined as to whether network traffic with aircraft is possible.

BzB Equipment (*)

BzB devices remain of little use in their present form. Tuning is difficult and inaccurate, also the device is very sensitive to vibrations; even with a suppressed engine, the ignition spark causes it to fail. In addition, the range of the device varies greatly and is subject to the curvature of the earth. Poor communication, excessively overloaded batteries, and frequent failures in the field make the unit unreliable and in need of improvement. A serviceable, reliable operating device with a minimum range of 10km would equip division command to control a march and maintain contact with scouting parties. The idea is to assign BzB devices to squadron leaders, in which case the 30W link to the main unit could be dropped. Captured French and British very high frequency (VHF) radios can be used as a pattern, since they are light and compact.

Armour protection for all radios including the 30W radio stations is essential for AufklAbt (mot).

Telephone Squad (cable)

The composition of the small telephone squad proved to be satisfactory. Instead of the *schweres Feldkabel* [heavy field cable], a lighter type would suffice and the overall length could be increased considerably. An interlocking rod with a cutting device for destroying enemy lines would greatly facilitate work during a rapid advance.

Weaponry and Equipment

The number of small arms is quite sufficient, a change does not appear to be fundamentally necessary. However, all platoon and squad leaders of the KradSchtz platoons, the heavy squadron and the *Panzerjäger Zug* [PzJgZg – anti-tank platoon] should be equipped with the 7.92mm *Maschinenpistole* [MP – machine pistole (submachine gun)] 38. For the KradSchtz platoons, it is imperative to supply them with the PzB.

Both the 7.92mm MG 34 and the 2cm KwK 30 L/55, have excellent effects. Any reservations are, in most cases, due to a lack of care of weapons and ammunition.

Ammunition for the MG 34 has had significantly more splits in steel cartridge cased bullets when compared to brass-cased type. The jamming occurred so frequently, that alternating fire protection by two deployed guns was not always guaranteed. In order to facilitate gunners No.4 and No.5 [ammunition carriers] to carry their rifles, it is proposed to introduce a back carrying device for two cartridge boxes.

The 2cm KwK 30 L/55 has proven itself in every respect and is greatly feared by the enemy. It is proposed to equip all PzSpWg except the SdKfz 223 with this weapon.

The present equipment of the KradSchtz platoons with the 5cm le GrWrf 36 is rejected. Instead, we consider the introduction of a platoon equipped with three to four 8cm *schwere Granatwerfer*s GrW – heavy mortar 34 to be appropriate. It is suggested that the AufklAbt (mot) be equipped as soon as possible with the more powerful 5cm PaK 39 instead of the 3.7cm PaK. The PzJgZg should be divided into two half platoons each equipped with two 5cm PaK and a 7.92mm MG 34.

The 7.5cm le IG 18 has proven itself fully, no proposed change.

Büssing-NAG Typ GS (*Achtrad*): The SdKfz 231, SdKfz 232 and SdKfz 263 have generally proved their worth. However, the following deficiencies still occur:

a.) The clutches are too weak. In a stock of 12 cars, they had to be replaced in two cases during service after some 2,500km, although Büssing-NAG had already replaced them with reinforced parts in October 1939.

b.) During the fighting, three axle joints had to be replaced. Central lubrication works unreliably and has failed in several cases.

c.) The vehicle is extremely sensitive to heat.

d.) The selector lever in the gearbox has been replaced or welded in four cases.

Horch *Typ* 801; The SdKfz 221, SdKfz 222 and SdKfz 223 used by the battalion have performed well. With a stock of 25 cars, the main faults encountered are as follows:

German infantry, including an MG team, pass a *gemischter Spähtrupp* of a AufklAbt (mot). The SdKfz 231 (6-Rad), to the left, confirms that an unknown number of the type remained in service during the French campaign. The weapons on all the vehicles are pointing skywards in anticipation of an attack by enemy aircraft.

a.) The bearing on the shaft for the steering operating lever is not up to the stress. It had to be replaced in three cases.

b.) The clutch as a whole is too weak and around six have been replaced. Some of the damage has been caused by a bad driving technique, which is due harsh use under combat conditions. This cannot be ruled out in the future. Some of this damage was also caused by jammed clutch plates on poorly lubricated shafts. We propose the installation of automatic lubrication.

c.) The clutch pedal operating lever is too weak. There were at least five or six breaks during use. The lever must be strengthened.

d.) The universal joints are too small and consequently weak. Six universal joint fractures occurred in use.

e.) The fastenings of the of the upper swing-arm suspension bracket to the chassis are too weak. Repairs proved to be very difficult. In most cases, the brackets were welded.

f.) In the transmission, the reverse and also the first and second gears are too weak. For this reason, four gears had to be replaced.

Superstructure: Numerous long cracks have appeared in the *Panzeraufbau* on many vehicles, especially those recently manufactured.

Tyres: Although described as 'bulletproof' they have proven to be the opposite; just a few hits by infantry ammunition renders a tyre not only immediately unusable, but also unrepairable. The only viable solution seems to be the Semperit-manufactured type with a solid rubber insert.

Passenger Cars: The medium all-terrain standard passenger car [Horch-built Kfz 12] has proven itself well. For the platoon leaders of the KradSchtz squadron it is proposed to equip them with a light off-road passenger car (Kfz 1 and Kfz 2) with four-wheel steering, since other passenger cars are too large and their mobility is insufficient. As a combat vehicle for the KradSchtz platoons, the Kfz 70 based on the Kfz 69 is proposed instead of the Kfz 18.

Trucks: The *Einheitsdiesel* [standardized diesel truck] has proven itself very well because of its exceptionally high tractive force, off-road capability and speed. Therefore, the uniform equipment with this type is desired.

Repairs: During the operation in the west the following damages were repaired: One *Achtrad* with three anti-tank hits to the front bulkhead with the forward steering completely destroyed and the suspension seriously damaged. One *Achtrad* with heavy shell damage to the side armour and also four light PzSpWg, with heavy shell damage to the side armour.

Some of the necessary equipment was captured by the PzAufklLehrAbt during the campaign. The urgently needed flat-bed trailer is still missing.

Conclusion: It has been noted that the patrols fight far more off-road in combat than they were taught in training. This ultimately placed very high demands on the off-road capabilities of our vehicles. During the French campaign, it was only due to good weather and ground conditions that the patrols were able to make good off-road progress. The introduction of a wheel-cum-track vehicle [Saurer RK 9] is therefore to be expedited. We expect this vehicle to provide significantly increased off-road capability at a slightly reduced speed.

(*) The *Bord-zu-Bord* (BzB) radio was planned as a universal device for all armoured vehicles. With a range of initially around 1km while driving and 2km when stationary, it was intended to provide communications within the companies/squadrons. At the time of its introduction, the official designation was *Funksprechtgerät* (FuSprechGer – radio telephone equipment) 'Ax'. At the time of its general introduction, this changed to FuSprechGer 'a'. An improved variant, the FuSprechGer 'b', was to be introduced in 1941. From 1942, the much more powerful FuSprechGer 'f' with a range of up to 8km became available.

(**) This complaint is difficult to understand, since it is precisely the open turret on the SdKfz 222 that allows better observation.

(***) This notation was almost prophetic. With the availability of the SdKfz 250 light armoured personnel carrier in 1942, the same procedure was to be followed.

(****) The mechanically sophisticated *Räder-Raupenfahrzeuge* (wheel-cum-track vehicles) of Austrian origin apparently made a lasting impression, and many German high-ranking officers demanded the introduction these vehicles.

After the campaign, the OKH sent a questionnaire to all Panzer divisions. The 7.PzDiv under General Erwin Rommel assessed the performance of the divisional reconnaissance elements completely differently:

In the early summer of 1941, a radio was successively fitted in all light and heavy armoured reconnaissance vehicles. The FuSprech 'a' transceiver had a range of only 1km when using a turret-mounted rod-type aerial. This SdKfz 231 is in service with the 7.PzDiv.

This SdKfz 263 was issued to 9.PzDiv. Since the roof hatches were not completely rainproof, a cover was fabricated to protect the sensitive radio equipment.

Question: Is an AufklAbt (mot) necessary for the Panzer divisions if independent armoured reconnaissance platoons are present in the Panzer brigade and rifle brigade? How should a PzAufklAbt be structured?

Reply: The division is in favour of unconditionally retaining the PzAufklAbt, even if the above proposed reconnaissance platoon is placed under the Schtz-Brig. The PzAufklAbt is the only organ of the PzDiv capable of long-range reconnaissance which is required after each breakthrough and during pursuit. The PzAufklAbt will be quite indispensable in the operation of a Panzer division for warfare in an eastern theatre [Soviet Union].

Nevertheless, the PzAufklAbt could not meet the requirements in most cases, neither in the Polish war nor in the Western campaign. The reason lies solely in the inadequacy of the reconnaissance vehicles. The armoured reconnaissance vehicle in its various forms is always tied to paved roads, and failed at all obstacles or enemy anti-tank defences. Its armour is so poor that it is not even safe against fire from 7.92mm SmK ammunition. This makes it inferior to all the enemy weapons. The tremendous loss of armoured reconnaissance vehicles already at the end of the first week of the Western campaign confirms this experience. On the eighth day of the operation, the

PzAufklAbt only had nine armoured reconnaissance vehicles. However, it would be wrong to conclude from this fact that the PzAufklAbt is of no value. Rather, for the division's indispensable ground-based reconnaissance tasks, it must be equipped with vehicles that enable it to break through enemy anti-tank defences or enemy barriers even on the battlefront.

During the western campaign, the PzAufklAbt, because of its high vehicle losses, was used only for the following tasks, and with great success:

a.) To reach and occupy important sections in front of and to the flanks of the division's advance, for which it is particularly capable because of its speed.

b.) To screen and consolidate the armoured attack.

c.) Flank protection.

The organization into two armoured reconnaissance companies, one motorcycle rifle company, and one heavy company, has proved fully effective and is considered sufficient. Reinforcement would only impair the manoeuvrability and mobility of the division. Specifically, the operation has demonstrated the need for the following changes:

June 1940: An SdKfz 222 leads a column of vehicles of an unknown PzDiv across the Marne as German forces advance from the Ardennes deeper into French territory.

a.) Radios must be available within the patrols. Previously, communication was by shouting or running across the battle area under enemy fire.

b.) A PaK platoon must be equipped with at least three 5cm PaK 38. The 2cm in the scout cars is not suitable for defence against enemy armoured vehicles.

c.) Detection equipment for the engineer platoon to clear mined roads quickly and without delay before the division arrives.

d.) A second heavy GrW group should be incorporated.

e.) Wheel-cum-track vehicles are called for to replace the conventional wheeled armoured reconnaissance vehicles. These should be capable of between 50kph to 60kph on the road with rubber-padded tracks. The armament should consist of a 2cm KwK 30 L/55 or a 4.7cm PaK in a turret, one to two MG should be able to fire to the front and rear.

The PzAufklAbt stands or falls on the development of a fully viable armoured reconnaissance vehicle.

This report shows a frightening misunderstanding of the tasks faced by the PzAufklAbt. It is true that offensive action is explicitly expected from the subunits attached to the battalion. However, the idea that reconnaissance vehicles could break through enemy lines was far from reality and also did not correspond to their operational principles.

The armour of the German reconnaissance vehicles was, due to their strength and shape, safe against fire with 7.92mm SmK ammunition at a range of over 50m. However, enemy anti-tank rifles and guns could easily penetrate them at virtually any range. The commanders of armoured reconnaissance vehicles must use skill to undermine the effect of enemy anti-tank weapons, and must retreat quickly in an emergency.

In the discussion it must not be forgotten that the German tanks also had only moderate frontal armour. All types, including the main battle tank of the 7.PzDiv, the PzKpfw 38(t), where (t) indicates *tschecisch* (Czechoslovak) origin, had a maximum frontal protection of 30mm during the Western campaign. An exception was the *Sturmgeschütz* (StuG – assault gun) with 50mm frontal armour. These were able to withstand considerably more hits.

Reinforcing the armour of the wheeled armoured reconnaissance vehicles to a level that would be safe against fire from anti-tank weapons would have pushed the weight to enormous heights. Apart from the fact that this was technically impossible (as of 1940), off-road mobility would have suffered greatly.

The 'tank-versus-anti-tank weapon' race was almost impossible to win. The demands for functioning short-range radios are understandable and comprehensible [see also the report of the PzAufklLehrAbt]. But in 1941, the battalions began to receive suitable equipment. Also, the wish for a more powerful anti-tank weapon for the heavy company was soon to be fulfilled. (Note, the traditional designation *Schwadron* [squadron]was slowly replaced by *Kompanie* [Kp – company] in the *Panzertruppe* [armoured force].)

A complete replacement of the wheeled armoured reconnaissance vehicles with other chassis concepts was not to be considered. The existing technology was to be used until the end of the war. In 1943, all eight-rad were to be replaced by a more powerful development.

France 1941: This SdKfz 232 (Fu) has been abandoned after all the tyres on one side have been punctured by enemy fire. The vehicle would be recovered to an engineer unit .

In the spring of 1941, the first German units were landed at Tripoli to support the hard-pressed Italian forces fighting in North Africa.

On 12 February 1941, 5.leDiv was reorganized by incorporating elements of 3.PzDiv and existing *Heerestruppen* (army troops) to form an armoured unit that was more comparable in structure to a conventional PzDiv than a light division of the pre-war era.

The AufklAbt 3 corresponded in its structure to a standard AufklAbt (mot). Originally only one PzSpKp was planned, but before shipping an additional *Aufklärungs-Zug* (AufklZg – reconnaissance platoon) issued with Volkswagen (*Typ* 87) was attached to the battalion. Nothing more is known about the exact composition of this platoon. It is interesting to note that for the first-time efforts were made to replace the motorcycle by a motor vehicle that was cheaper to produce and more versatile [see Chapter 8] .

In addition, 5.leDiv was supported by *leichtes Infanterie-Regiment* (le InfRgt – light infantry regiment) 200 (also called *Schützen-Regiment* [SchtzRgt – rifle regiment] 200). The regiment unusually had two *Maschinengewehr-Bataillonen* (MGBtl – machine-gun battalions) – MGBtl 2 and MGBtl 8 – in place of the usual *Schützen-Bataillonen* (SchtzBtl – rifle battalions). According to official files, an additional 20 SdKfz 251 were also issued. Due to the overall high firepower, elements of this unit were often assigned to support the AufklAbt 3.

Shortly time later, 15.PzDiv arrived at Tripoli. This was also a regular tank division (as of 1941) with only one tank regiment (PzRgt 15) with two battalions. The *Schützen-Brigade* (SchtzBde – rifle brigade) consisted of two regiments each with two battalions. In addition, another KradSchtzBtl was assigned to the brigade. This also could effectively support the reconnaissance division. The AufklAbt 33 was of the normal standard.

Opposite: A SdKfz 223 of the 5.leDiv in North Africa. The frame-type antenna is erected, and four 1.25m *Steckantenne* (plug-in aerial) have been fitted together to make a 5m support for a *Sternantenne* 'a'. Presumably, the 80W transmitter (Fu 12) was able to reach its maximum range of up to 160km when stationary.

Due to the special climatic and terrain characteristics of North Africa, the deployment of the reconnaissance units on the desert battlefield was different to that in the European theatre of war. Here, too, typical reconnaissance squads were initially issued with two to three PzSpWg. Since some of these vehicles were not fitted with radio equipment, a PzSpWg (Fu) – either a SdKfz 223 or

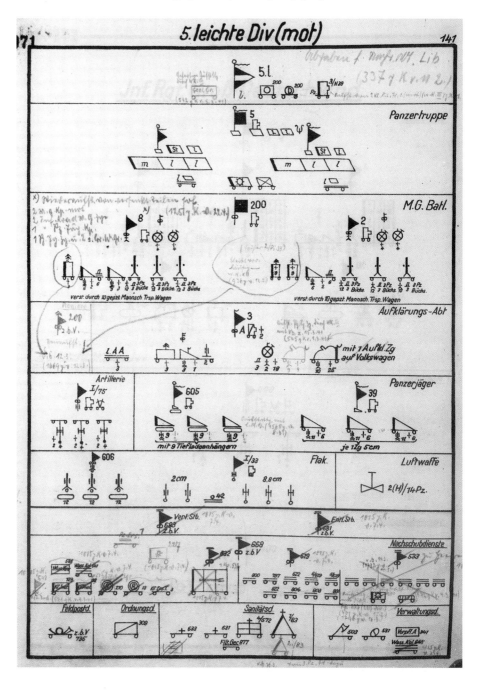

The organizational structure for 5.leDiv. In addition to the armoured reconnaissance vehicles, the PzSpKp had a *Kübelwagen*-equipped reconnaissance platoon.

a SdKfz 232 – always had to be present. The reconnaissance division was forced to adapt to the situation.

On 18 October 1941, *Hauptmann* Daumiller wrote to the special staff department 'Felmy' of *Fremde Heeres West* (Foreign Armies West), revealing interesting details about his own reconnaissance units as well as those of the British:

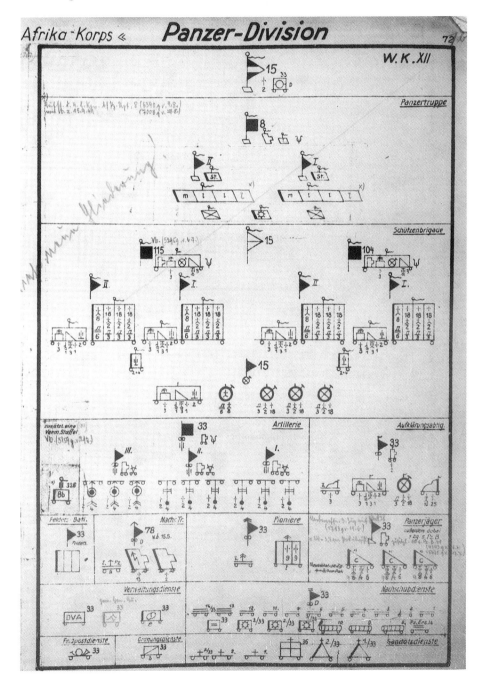

The reconnaissance elements of the 15.PzDiv were similarly equipped.

Each of the units deployed to North Africa as reinforcements at the end of 1942 were issued with the SdKfz 233 for the heavy platoons in their reconnaissance units. The 7.5cm KwK L/24 gun gave them the firepower to make limited offensive advances.

Tactical experience in combat

Reconnaissance squads consisted in the majority of an armoured reconnaissance squad and one or two anti-tank guns. Since in most cases these squads are deployed over distances of up to 200km, it is important that their vehicles match the lower speeds of the gun tractors. In contact with enemy armoured reconnaissance vehicles, it became apparent that they quickly recognized the PaK as it was being moved into a firing position. Then, taking advantage of his high speed, he quickly withdrew out of range and then halted again and continued to observe our positions. As soon as the PaK tried to approach within a favourable firing distance, the British scouting party would move out range. It turned out that, despite being less manoeuvrable, the 5cm guns with their longer range of fire were the most suitable for such operations. During the operations by the patrols, only the 5cm PaK was successful. Despite their high speed, Humber scout cars were destroyed at ranges over 600m.

When our reconnaissance troops approached entrenched British positions, the enemy immediately sent his own armoured reconnaissance vehicles to meet ours. These were able to effectively direct the fire of the British artillery. During many of our

scouting attacks, the British would veer away in the direction of their positions in order to draw our scout cars into the effective range of his artillery.

In general, the British scout cars have great admiration for the towed 5cm PaK L/60. Despite its heavy weight, the weapon is the preferred gun for scouting parties if it is brought into position very quickly by an efficient crew. The gun shields on both the 5cm PaK and the 3.7cm PaK were not penetrated by either rifle fire or shell fragments.

The Volkswagen *Typ* 82, commonly known as the *Kübelwagen* (bucket seat vehicle), was popular with reconnaissance detachments in North Africa. The report of AufklAbt 3 continues:

Motor vehicles
The main enemy of the motor vehicle in the desert is the fine sand, which resulted in very high wear despite oil bath-type filters and good sealing. The engine in a number of our Volkswagens had to be replaced after only 5,000km, whereas others have run 12,000km without any problems. Therefore, the care of the motor vehicles must become

The SdKfz 232 was equipped with a Fu 12 radio to ensure radio communication with the staff of the PzDiv. The *Zerscheller-Platte* served as a convenient storage space for baggage and jerrycans of water.

General Fritz Bayerlein, the chief of staff of the *Deutsche Afrika Korps* (DAK) in his Kfz 15 staff car. He was assisted by a corps intelligence detachment, and the SdKfz 263 (Fu) was used to maintain radio communications with elements of the reconnaissance detachment operating some distance ahead.

a priority. A driver, who regularly and carefully maintains his car on his own initiative, can significantly increase its life span, especially that of the engine. Engine damage due to clogging of the fuel supply and dirt and sand in carburettors occurs very frequently. The tank, fuel lines and carburettor must be thoroughly cleaned from time to time. According to reports, the filters have also been improved.

The *Kübelwagen* has performed outstandingly well. This verdict is received from every quarter. For driving in the desert, the reconnaissance department fitted the wide, low-pressure [balloon] tyres without treads. With these tyres, even tracks through deep sand are no longer obstacle. Rock-strewn slopes could be driven over with much less vibration than with the hard, narrow high-pressure tyre.

By comparison, the British wheeled vehicles and trucks have wider tyres of larger diameter, but they have a heavy tread pattern. The enemy does not seem to use twin tyres on his trucks. On our vehicles, a lot of damage has occurred with this arrangement due to rocks becoming jammed between the two tyres.

The intense sunlight leads to an increase in air pressure, which can cause the inner tube to burst and many repair patches leak. Therefore, great importance was attached to covering the tyres, including the spare. The last vehicles to arrive at the DAK had roll-up canvas flaps mounted on the mudguards, which could be lowered over the tyres. When available, passenger buses were used as command vehicles at all staff levels. Unlike tents, these vehicles permit working even in a sandstorm and without the ever-present swarm of flies.

The material situation of the *Deutsche Afrika Korps* (DAK) fluctuated greatly. The strategy, both offensive and defensive, adopted by Rommel was dependent on replacement supplies from the Reich. But the delivery of supplies varied widely; attacks by aircraft of the RAF and Royal Navy warships and submarines made it difficult for Axis convoys to cross the Mediterranean. As a result, the Germans were forced to use very large numbers of vehicles and equipment captured from the enemy. Among these were armoured cars.

In their morning and evening reports, the armoured divisions generally gave only the situation of the Panzer battalions (target, actual, and losses).

The 5.leDiv, renamed the 21.PzDiv on 1 August 1941, issued a report regarding its AufklAbt on 29 December 1941:

Type	Target	Actual	Missing
Beiwagen-Kräder	130	16	114
Kfz 1/ VW Typ 82	26	12	14
SdKfz 221	10	3	7
SdKfz 222	14	3	11
SdKfz 223	4	1	3
SdKfz 231	3	1	2
SdKfz 232	3	0	3
SdKfz 260	1	0	1
SdKfz 261	4	1	3
SdKfz 263	3	1	2
SdKfz 247	2	0	2

The high proportion of *Beiwagen-Kräder* is interesting. However, of the 130 assigned vehicles, only a little more than ten percent were present. The officially assigned armoured scout cars and armoured radio cars clearly exceeded the numbers given in KStN 1162. The allocation of SdKfz 260 and SdKfz 261 were not covered in the tables.

On 13 February 1942, AufklAbt 33 (15.PzDiv) reported one SdKfz 223 and four SdKfz 222 still in its PzSpKp, some 20 percent of the target strength of 25 light PzSpWg and heavy PzSpWg.

Fighting in the arid, treeless expanse of the North African desert battlefront often necessitated that tactics be adapted. Another report delivered by

Above: The dry terrain of the North African desert enabled the reconnaissance units to use the speed and cross-country performance to full effect. This mixed reconnaissance unit has only one armoured vehicle, an SdKfz 223, which served as a radio station.

Right: The *Einheits-Sehklappen* (standardized vision visors) indentify this as a second series SdKfz 231 (8-Rad). The vehicle is in service with the AufklAbt of 15.PzDiv.

AufklAbt 3 (21.PzDiv, formerly 5.leDiv) in August 1942 relentlessly exposes its own problems with regard to materiel and equipment.

Field report on the enemy and own AufklDiv (mot)

I.) Combat methods of the enemy reconnaissance forces, their motor vehicles and weapons: In contrast to the previous year and this spring, enemy reconnaissance forces appeared to be almost exclusively with assigned self-propelled anti-tank guns [Ordnance Quick Firing (OQF) 2-Pounder gun on a 15cwt light truck: Gun *Portée*].

The new British Humber Mk II armoured car mounts a 15mm Besa heavy machine gun [Czechoslovak-designed ZB-60], which can penetrate the armour on our cars at 1,500m range. Since the German 2cm KwK 30 L/55 cannon can only penetrate the Humber at less than 800m range, our own cars are vulnerable. This inferiority was compensated by reinforcing our own patrols with captured weapons.

Unlike our PzSpWg, all British armoured cars are equipped with radio, giving their crews an advantage. It is possible for the enemy to deploy the cars individually for reconnaissance and security over a wide area. The radio equipment allows trained soldiers to direct the fire of the attached artillery battery.

II.) Own way of fighting, suggestions for improvement: To continue to enforce effective

Towards the end of 1942, light armoured personnel carriers began to be delivered to units in North Africa. This SdKfz 250/1, camouflaged with sand-yellow stripes, carries a 7.92mm heavy MG 34. The stone-strewn terrain of Tunisia caused the rubber track pads to wear out at an alarming rate.

reconnaissance, a larger number of self-propelled guns are needed. The enemy fears the fire of our 4.7cm PaK mounted on a PzKpfw I.

The 2cm KwK 30 L/55 is no longer sufficient. It is proposed to equip the fast and effective eight-wheel reconnaissance vehicle with a 5cm KwK L/60 and an MG 42. The latter must also be able to be used for protection against low-flying aircraft. Since the car can also be steered backwards, a traverse of 60 degrees is sufficient for the turret. In this sense, the latest *Achtradwagen* [8-wheeled vehicle (SdKfz 233)] armed with a 7.5cm 37 KwK L/24, will reinforce the scout troops, will certainly prove effective. From a purely mechanical point of view, it can be said that the air filter and radiator, which were constantly malfunctioning, need further improvement. No faults were found on the chassis and any other problems were repaired by the engineers. Larger tyres would be beneficial, and off-road capability could be significantly increased. The size of the vehicle did not prove to be a disadvantage, thanks to its height it provides good observation. With their long range, manoeuvrability, and rapid fire, the British 8.76cm [OQF 25-Pounder field gun/howitzer] has proved to be an excellent weapon.

Opposite: In 1942, the first 7.5cm-armed SdKfz 233 entered service with the DAK. The PzAufklAbt now had a highly mobile heavy weapon that could be deployed to reinforce armoured reconnaissance squads. The 7.5cm *Kanone* (K – gun) 37 L/24 fired high-explosive or shaped-charge ammunition and also smoke shells.

The performance of the British 15mm Besa heavy machine gun cannot be verified. This appeared to have been superior to the 2cm *Panzergranate* (PzGr – armour-piercing tank shell) 40. The practice of loading anti-tank guns on trucks was also very effective; this indicates that a large proportion of the Gun *Portées* captured from the British were used by German forces. Also, a 2cm FlaK 38 L/55 on a SdKfz 10/4 half-track tractor and other improvised solutions on trucks were used by the AufklAbt with much success.

PzJgAbt 650 was attached to 21.PzDiv (formerly 5.leDiv), which had 27 PzKpfw I mounting a 4.7cm PaK(t). In order to improve tactical mobility and to spare the chassis of the old PzKpfw I, nine flat-bed trailers were assigned to the PzJg unit and these were regularly made available to AufklAbt 3.

The equipping of the German armoured reconnaissance vehicles with the FuSprech 'a' radio was not to begin until mid-1941. Here the British seemed to have had the advantage; it is interesting to note their practice of allowing reconnaissance units to direct artillery fire. This required good radio equipment.

It is not known whether the German PzSpWg-equipped units fitted radios at field or base workshops. Vehicles shipped to North Africa in 1942 as replacements were most certainly equipped with FuSprech 'a' or 'd'.

Additional units were sent to North Africa as reinforcements. In November 1941, the first units of what later became the 90.*leichte Afrika Division* were formed. From April 1942 the unit, now 90.leDiv, reached its full strength with three motorized armoured infantry regiments and an armoured division. The reconnaissance elements (as of November 1942) consisted of the mixed AufklAbt 580 with an armoured reconnaissance company, a heavy armoured

This SdKfz 223 (Fu) served as a relay vehicle for the staff echelons in a PzDiv. The lightly armoured vehicle was used to maintain contact between front-line reconnaissance units and the commanders of their battalion. The PzKpfw II is in service with light platoon of a PzAbt.

reconnaissance platoon with six SdKfz 233 [see Chapter 8], a support company, and also a battery of light field howitzers.

In 1943, the *Afrika Division* 999 was transferred to North Africa. The infantry division had a AufklAbt (mot) with a standard armoured reconnaissance company, a heavy armoured reconnaissance platoon with six SdKfz 233 [see Chapter 8], and also two heavy companies.

In view of the deteriorating situation in North Africa, 10.PzDiv was transferred to Tunisia in December 1942. After reforming in France, the unit initially had a mixed KradSchtz battalion, which corresponded to a strong AufklAbt in terms of organization. But in March 1943, it was reorganized as a PzAufklAbt.

Right: From mid-1942, the s PzSpWg was slightly modified. The shape of the front armour plate was simplified and the thickness increased from 14.5mm to 30mm. This SdKfz 231 was transferred to Tunisia, at the end of 1942, with PzSpKp 287 in *Sonderverband* (SVerb – special duties) 287.

Below: An SdKfz 222 which was delivered to Tunisia in late November 1942. It carries the marking for 10.PzDiv and served with the reconnaissance battalion.

Above: A patrol of two SdKfz 222 near the frontline. In 1942, the more powerful 2cm KwK 38 L/55 began to be fitted which made the light and mechanically simple vehicle even more effective in desert conditions.

Left: A SdKfz 263, operating as a long-range radio communications section.

Soviet Union 7

With the start of *Unternehmen* (Operation) *Barbarossa*, 17 Panzer divisions attacked the Soviet Union. Other highly mobile units included several from the SS and ten motorized infantry divisions.

In July 1941, PzAufklAbt 5 (2.PzDiv) submitted an interesting report. In March 1941, the division had participated in the Balkan campaign and in May the division was deployed to Lemberg-Przemysl in Poland. When the Russian campaign began on 22 June, 1941, the division initially remained in Poland as an OKH reserve. Here, captured Red Army tanks, which were shipped to Poland in July 1941, were used for ballistics tests:

Field report regarding the instructional firing by 1./PzAufklAbt 5 at Sadow-Wiczenia on 24 July 1941

The company conducted a test and instructional firing on Russian armoured fighting vehicles of the types T-26A (Vickers-Armstrong, 8.5t), type T-26C (Vickers-Armstrong, 9.7t) and the Soviet-built type T-35 (five turrets). Shooting was done at different ranges with 2cm KwK 30 L/55 and 2cm KwK 38 L/55 as well as a 7.92mm PzB 39. The following results were obtained:

Target, T-26C (*),
Firing 2cm PzGr, range 500m.
Front armour: Vertical driver's front hatch with reinforced vision visor was shot through. Armour was not penetrated.

Turret front: Gun front hatch clean penetrations, turret armour behind was not penetrated.

Hull and turret side: At an impact angle of between 70 to 90 degrees had no effect and ricocheted off, clear penetrations of the 25mm armour were achieved. All shots

Opposite: An assembled propaganda image of a FliVO standing in an SdKfz 261 and directing a flight of *Luftwaffe* Junkers Ju-87 StuKa dive bombers to their target. (Getty)

Yugoslavia in 1941: Elements of a German reconnaissance unit, part of the force deployed to suppress the Racan militia, patrol through the town of Bajina Bašta. The leading vehicle is an SdKfz 232 (6-Rad), followed by a modified Tatra OA vz 30, which had been commandeered from the Czechoslovak army.

hitting the armoured fighting vehicle at an angle of impact of less than 70 degrees ricocheted off the armour.

Target, T-35
Firing with 2cm PzGr range 120m.
All turrets (large main turret with 7.62cm gun, two small turrets with 4.5cm gun long, two small turrets with MG) were smoothly penetrated on all sides. When hit in the main turret about 10cm to the left of reinforced mantlet, a fire started inside the vehicle, first visible by a black cloud of smoke, later by bright red glowing flame. Since it was still fully equipped with ammunition, it was not possible to exactly note the results, since there was danger of an explosion.

Target, attempt, T-35
Firing by PzB 39, range 100m.
Front armour: The frontal armour below the front right turret was easily penetrated. These hits would have mortally wounded the gunner at the level of the abdomen. The reinforced driver's view hatch as well as the nose armour was not penetrated.

MG turret, 4.5cm gun turret, 7.62cm main turret: The turrets were clearly penetrated, but not the gun ports. The crews of the turrets would have been put out of action.

Hull side armour: The armour over the running gear was easily penetrated, but had no effect because the hull armour behind them was not penetrated.

Summary: The types fired on by the company have been penetrated with 2cm ammunition in some places at up to 500m, and in all places at up to 300m. Naturally,

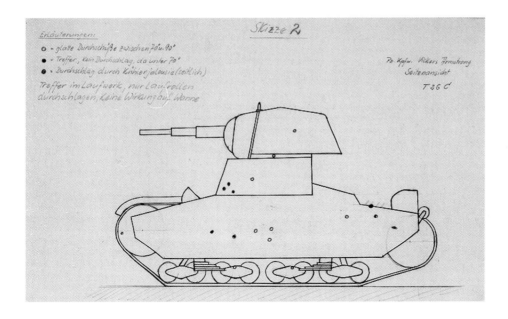

the effect increased as the range was decreased. The gunners have gained confidence in their weapons and due to this test firing they have overcome the *Panzerschreck* (tank shock). In the hands of a steadfast gunner, the PzB 39 is an extremely effective weapon, capable of penetrating even the heaviest Russian tank. The fighting power of the tank, if it is not completely put out of action, is considerably reduced by wounding members of the crew.

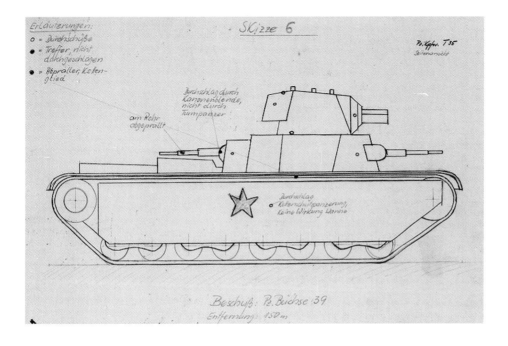

Yugoslavia 1943: Soon after the swift conclusion of the Balkan campaign, a bloody partisan war began which forced the OKH to deploy occupation troops. Here an SdKfz 222, armed with a 2cm KwK 38 L/55, provides fire support for an infantry unit.

(*) The T-26C is the German designation for the T-26 M1938 with slightly slanted armour. Firing tests at 300m resulted in clear penetrations throughout, even at the front.

There is not much to add to the remarks made by the commander of PzAukflAbt 5. After a short stay in France as an occupation force, the unit was transferred to the central section of the Eastern Front in September 1941. At that time PzAufklAbt 5 was merged with SchtzBtl 2 and its former 1.Kp became 4./KradSchtzBtl 2.

The trials showed that the German armoured reconnaissance vehicles armed with 2cm KwK 30 L/55, all pre-war developments, could safely engage the Russian tanks produced during this period. Even 'heavy' tanks like the T-35 were not safe. However, it should not be forgotten that these had a maximum armour thickness of 30mm. The surprising appearance of the modern T-34 and KV-1 made the results of these firing tests obsolete. In action against these tanks, the weapons of the reconnaissance division were practically ineffective.

On 22 September 1941, the ObdH published a brief report:

Experiences of the Eastern Campaign

Again and again, the importance of sufficient combat reconnaissance must be emphasized. Particularly in the case of inadequate air reconnaissance, this is of increased importance. Often the Russians let reconnaissance units through or opened well-aimed infantry fire at close ranges. This often resulted in high losses of officers and enlisted men. Therefore, reconnaissance units must be sufficiently strong and equipped with heavy weapons. These must be supervised in their action by the main forces and provided with adequate fire protection.

A Russian statement about German reconnaissance states the following: German reconnaissance vehicles are poorly camouflaged and move conspicuously. Our observers can recognize and follow them easily. Enemy reconnaissance forces always move out of their positions alone and travel along the same path, instead of trying to deceive us by changing their route.

As a result of what was becoming a war of attrition on the *Ost* (East) Front, the previous organization, equipment and armament of the reconnaissance elements in the armoured divisions was called into question.

On 13 September 1941, PzAufklAbt 13 submitted a proposal to the division command for the formation of a reinforced PzAufklAbt:

Shortly after the conclusion of the Balkan campaign, the long-planned and repeatedly postponed invasion of Soviet Union began. These vehicles of the AufklLehrAbt – a SdKfz 231 and a SdKfz 232, drive over a bridge assembled from *Brückengerät* 'K' sections to cross the Berezina, near Bobruisk.

An SdKfz 232 (8-Rad), closely followed by an SdKfz 221, is being driven cautiously through a battle scarred town during *Unternehmen Marita* as German forces advance on Greece.

Above: An SdKfz 232 in service with the reconnaissance squad from PzAufklAbt 59 (8.PzDiv) travel through a Russian village.

Right: A *Kradmelder* (dispatch rider). He wears a regulation long, leather motor-cycle coat, heavy leather gloves, and a gas mask container. A vital battery-powered torch is buttoned on the coat.

The proposals are based on the experience gained from three independent reconnaissance missions and also from those PzAufklAbt with KradSchtzBtl with the combat group. The combat strength of the PzAufklAbt in its previous structure: staff, signals platoon, a PzSpKp armoured reconnaissance company, a KradSchtzKp and the *Trosse* [(supply) trains] has proven to be inadequate. The battalion always had to be assigned reinforcements from other elements of the PzDiv when it was given combat or security missions, if not I was ordered to establish a combat group with other units. In order that the PzAufklAbt can absolutely carry out its reconnaissance tasks and also be used as a combat arm of the Panzer division, we propose a reorganization.

The structure would be as follows:

- *Abteilungsstab* (battalion staff)
- *Nachrichten-Zug* (signals platoon)
- 1.PzSpKp (armoured reconnaissance company)
- 2.KradSchtzKp and 3.KradSchtzKp (motorcycle rifle companies)
- *Schützen-Kompanie* (rifle company)
- *schwere Kompanie* (heavy company)
- *leichte Kolonne* (light column)
- *Instandsetzungs-Staffel* (workshop section)

The staff remains unchanged, requiring only one additional officer.

The signals platoon does not have to be reorganized, but only supplied with an additional equipment corresponding to the enlargement of the battalion. This can, however, be taken for the most part from the inventory of the KradSchtzBtl.

The decision to maintain only one PzSpKp instead of two is maintained. However, the previous number of PzSpWg of 24 plus one radio post (*) per company has proved insufficient. Under the present conditions and in view of the experience gained, 30 armoured cars plus one radio post are required.

Justification: It must be possible to conduct a rollover operation with due regard for the material, and there should also always be a certain reserve of armoured reconnaissance vehicles. This objective is achieved by forming up to 12 reconnaissance squads. Three reconnaissance squads are needed for front-line reconnaissance, and two squads are required for flank reconnaissance (average 12 to 13 PzSpWg). A further reconnaissance unit with two or three cars serve as a direct reserve. The armoured vehicles not used in reconnaissance squads were successfully deployed for leading the vanguard, as liaison vehicles to the main squad, and for air cover on the march.

At present, with a target of 24 armoured reconnaissance vehicles, not even the front-line squads are operational because, in addition to losses due to enemy action, many vehicles had broken down due to mechanical fatigue (the division today still has vehicles built in 1936).

Furthermore, a different breakdown of the types is demanded and the emphasis should be on the type SdKfz 222, with a closed turret and armed with the new KwK 40 would be desirable. (**)

The KradSchtzKp has proven itself very well as such in the PzAufklAbt. The prerequisite is be issued with dedicated equipment (750cc Zündapp). Its division into three KradSchtzZg has proven successful. The 5cm GrW 36 has practically never been used because its range of 200m to 500m is too short. The 8cm GrW 34 has not only a longer range, but also a much better effect on the target. Each KradSchtzKp should be equipped with a heavy MG group and a heavy GrW group as a 4.*Zug* under the command of an officer. This measure increases the combat value of the company. The necessary heavy GrW are available at the KradSchtzBtl. Furthermore, we propose to replace the motorcycle combination with the all-terrain *Kübelwagen*. Besides the better off-road capability

A SdKfz 232 of PzAufklAbt 27 (17.PzDiv) is cautiously driven through a cornfield. This could be very hazardous, since Soviet close-combat fighters could be hiding in the tall grain.

Vehicles of a AufklAbt pass elements of a horse-drawn unit. In the first months of *Unternehmen Barbarossa*, large air recognition banners were obligatory because of German air superiority.

thanks to the all-wheel drive, and essential components are effectively protected. Inside the vehicle, the weapons and equipment, are no longer exposed to the elements. Moreover, the vehicle is small and easy to camouflage. (***)

The SchtzKp, similar in structure to the KradSchtzKp is to be loaded onto all-terrain trucks.

The heavy company remains as before with the infantry gun platoon and the engineer platoon. The PaK platoon, on the other hand, must be reinforced. As with PzJgAbt 13, the mounting of a 3.7cm PaK on a SdKfz 10, as a makeshift self-propelled gun carriage, has generally proved successful. The only 3.7cm PaK in the PzAufklAbt, was made mobile in this way, and knocked-out 11 enemy tanks in two days. Our two towed PaK knocked-out four and five respectively. It also has the advantage of being able to be used as an assault gun. We request that the number of 3.7cm PaK be increased to six (two as self-propelled guns and four towed). In addition, two 5cm PaK must be made available to take the fight to heavier tanks.

(*) The radio station (*mittlerer Funktrupp* 'b' [mot]) is an armoured radio car [SdKfz 263] with long-range 100W radio equipment. The other armoured reconnaissance vehicles were probably not yet equipped with the BzB system (FuSprech 'a' or 'd' transceiver).

(**) This can only be wishful thinking. A closed turret was never planned for the light PzSpWg. The 'KwK 40' weapon cannot be identified, it will not have been the 7.5cm KwK 40 introduced in 1942.)

(***) This reference is puzzling. The mentioned "Volkswagen with all-wheel drive" can only be VW Type 82, which actually had only rear-wheel drive. The Type 166 *Schwimmwagen* (swimming car) was not to go into series production until autumn 1942.

The proposal of the commander of PzAufklAbt 13 amounts, in principle, to a merger of the KradSchtzBtl and the PzAufklAbt; this began to take place in 1942.

The Panzer divisions each had a light tank platoon at regimental and battalion level, which was available to an individual commander. As of November 1941, a light platoon was normally issued with six PzKpfw II, which performed a variety of tasks, including close reconnaissance, independent of the reconnaissance detachment in a PzDiv. A field report of PzRgt 35 (4.PzDiv) from February 1942 reveals some interesting details:

The PzKpfw II is unsuitable as a reconnaissance tank due to its thin armour, inadequate armament and poor visibility. Where it was used for reconnaissance in the Eastern campaign, it usually suffered heavy losses. After a short time, no more tanks were available. A suitable reconnaissance tank should, importantly, be so heavily armoured that enemy PaK could not harm the vehicle. The second requirement is for speed and mobility, a much higher speed for the majority of the tanks in the regiment would be necessary. Whereas, effective firepower is of secondary importance; we propose a machine gun and a 2.8cm s PzB 41. Since such an armoured vehicle is not expected in the short term, the PzKpfw II will have to continue to be used. Since the periscopes in the turret roof have failed, we propose the vehicle is fitted with the same of *Panzerführer-Kuppel* [commander's cupola] as used on the PzKpfw III.

April 1941: An SdKfz 232 (8 – Rad) and an SdKfz 222 on patrol after German forces successfully occupied Yugoslavia. Both vehicles are in service with the reconnaissance battalion in SS-PzDiv *Liebstandarte* Adolf Hitler.

This assessment reflects the desire of many commanding officers for the

An SdKfz 263 (Fu) from the NachrAbt of 7.PzDiv. The 1.4m rod-type antenna indicates that the vehicle has been fitted with a FuSprech 'a' transceiver. The well-loaded vehicle has been fitted with two horns and, for some reason, a motorcycle is carried on the rear.

perfect combat vehicle. In this context, perhaps understandably, the focus for tank crewmen is often on the most effective armour. At the beginning of the war, however, the HWA set other priorities: reconnaissance vehicles were to have high mobility, a manageable size, and good means of observation and radio communication. By 1941, development of reconnaissance tanks was at an advanced stage, and the first types became available in 1942. For various reasons, large-scale deliveries to front-line units did not to take place.

Instead, from the end of 1942 the PzKpfw III was initially issued to light tank platoons attached to, for example, *schwere Panzerabteilungen* (s PzAbt – heavy tank [*Tiger*] battalions). With the introduction of the standard 'Panzer Division 43', the platoons of the tank regiments or tank divisions, now became reconnaissance platoons and were to be equipped with the PzKpfw IV or PzKpfw V *Panther*. These at least fulfilled the request made by crewmen for better armour. Both types could be used as a reserve for the Panzer divisions.

An unusually large number of field reports from PzAufklAbt 13 have been preserved in the archives. On 18 January 1942, the commander answered a comprehensive list of questions:

Special experience in scouting service

The principles contained in the regulations on the employment and conduct of reconnaissance have proven themselves. Once again it has been shown that tactical reconnaissance in the divisional combat area should be performed by only the PzAufklAbt. Individual reconnaissance detachments should never be attached to other combat units or formations. However, the performance of reconnaissance tasks was limited by the number of operational vehicles available at a given time.

The equipment of the PzAufklAbt with armoured reconnaissance vehicles according to the currently valid KStN is insufficient, especially with regard to the old PzSpWg, which were already mechanically tired at the beginning of the Eastern campaign. In addition to the mechanical failures, many were lost due to enemy action. During the Eastern campaign, only *Panzerspäh-Truppen* (PzSpTrp – armoured reconnaissance squads) were used for tactical operations over larger areas, not KradSchtz reconnaissance squads. The mission and terrain, as well as the type and number of operational reconnaissance vehicles, determine the composition of the armoured squadrons. In principle, each reconnaissance squad must be equipped with an armoured, all-terrain radio vehicle, except for specialized close-range reconnaissance. Of great importance is the provision of at least one armour-piercing weapon.

Vehicles of the AufklLehrAbt in 1.KavDiv. The SdKfz 222 in the foreground carries the badge of 24.PzDiv – a leaping horseman in an open circle.

In the east, for a regular mission, reconnaissance squads issued with three armoured reconnaissance vehicles – one le PzSpWg [SdKfz 222], one le PzSpWg [SdKfz 221] and one le PzSpWg (Fu) [SdKfz 223] – proved effective in the formation of an armoured division. The allocation of a second SdKfz 222 should be sought. Such equipment would have facilitated fighting in Ukraine, but this was not possible due to the equipment situation. If necessary, and always with great success, two armoured reconnaissance squads would operate together in a *Breitkeil* [wedge] formation and advance deeper into enemy territory. The SdKfz 221, SdKfz 222 and SdKfz 223 proved better than the SdKfz 231 (8-Rad) and SdKfz 232 (8-Rad). It is essential that all armoured reconnaissance vehicles are fitted with BzB equipment.

Mixed, reinforced tank scouting parties were almost invariably used for aggressive reconnaissance. If the division could not provide support elements, the KradSchtzKp were called in. The reconnaissance squads then consisted of a SdKfz 222, a SdKfz 223 (Fu) and a KradSchtzZg, reinforced by a 3.7cm PaK. During this type of operation, the assignment of a 7.5cm le IG 18 was essential. Also, instead of a towed anti-tank gun, a PaK mounted on an SdKfz 10 proved to be very effective.

An SdKfz 250/3 from the staff section AufklLehrAbt. A tripod fitted with a barely camouflaged *Scherenfernrohr* (scissors telescope) has been mounted on the superstructure. Note the frame-type antenna has a non-standard central bar.

Reconnaissance units consisting only of PzSpWg can ensure the necessary close cooperation, but only when BzB radios were available. In case of mixed patrols and reinforced patrols, solo motorcycles are used to maintain communication between PzSpWg and the combat unit.

This SdKfz 222 carries the divisional sign for 16.PzDiv and the tactical sign for a reconnaissance company. The vehicle has been fitted with additional frontal armour.

KradSchtz reconnaissance units proved their worth only for combat reconnaissance with limited targets. Since they are not equipped with the necessary signaling equipment, the units can only be deployed for close-range or definitive combat reconnaissance. During the advance through Ukraine, the vast fields of wheat, corn and sunflowers caused many problems; they obscured the view of the KradSchtz. Furthermore, the dust was such that only the leading vehicle had a clear view of the terrain ahead. Not only do the KradSchtz see little but, due to loud engine noise, they also hear nothing. All of which makes them extremely vulnerable. Without being accompanied by armoured scout cars, the KradSchtz would quickly be halted by enemy fire. A KradSchtz scouting party over long distances can neither fully nor quickly fulfill its orders. In the event of mechanical problems, which occurred very often as a result of the terrain, the crew of the *Beiwagen-Kräder* is more or less helpless unless they can solve the problem.

Weapons: The 5cm le GrW 36 has lost its importance as a complementary medium-range weapon for a PzAufklAbt in the mobile warfare of the Eastern campaign. A supply of the 8cm s GrW 34 is vitally important.

The 5.PzDiv was not deployed for the invasion of the Soviet Union, but remained in Greece until the end of May. In June 1941, the division was re-equipped near Berlin and then moved east in September.

The heavy MG 34 was not used with its periscopic aiming device during the attack operations in the east. During trench warfare in the winter months, this will once again be important, since the heavy MG can cover large areas from prepared positions at the rear. At night, the heavy MG was used at prominent points such as tracks, bridges, and village streets to good effect. The prerequisite, however, was that they were carefully set up and prepared for instant action.

The PzB 39 and s PzB 41 have in no way met with requirements. Since their penetrating power is insufficient they can be removed.

Before the war, attempts were made to tow light infantry guns or PaK with motorcycle [Zundapp 750cc] with a driven sidecar. On the Russian gravel-surfaced roads, or even a

One of the ten SdKfz 247 Ausf A built in 1937. The vehicles were only assigned to the commander of a reconnaissance battalion. However, this vehicle carries the pennant (a black cross on a pink background) of a division commander.

The 2cm KwK 30 mounted in the SdKfz 222 almost filled the tank shield, which meant neither the driver nor the gunner (visible here) had little freedom to move. The treacherous terrain, covered with tree stumps, made it difficult to use the light armoured reconnaissance vehicle.

hard surface, any attempt would be futile. As a towing vehicle, the SdKfz 10 half-track proved to be the best. In desperate situation, even *Einheitsdiesel* [standardized diesel] trucks were used to tow the guns. In emergencies, armoured reconnaissance vehicles could be used to tow this type of gun.

Radio equipment: The PzAufklAbt must be reinforced by two Kfz 17-mounted light radio troop 'b' radio squads and also a heavy telephone cable-laying section.

The 100W and 30W radios have proved serviceable and are up to the task. The portable *Tornister-Funkgeräte* 'b', on the other hand, lacks range. In addition, the type is too vulnerable to the weather and terrain conditions which affect performance and, importantly, reliability. This must be significantly improved for future operational use.

The FunkSprechGer 'a' transceiver basically proved its worth in the PzSpTrp. Initially difficulties arose due to the poor installation of the equipment which began to be fitted at the launch of the campaign and continued, when time allowed, during the first weeks of operations.

The performance in the scouting units was satisfactory after the installation had been checked by specialists and the crews had become accustomed to the equipment. However, the FuSprech 'a' did not prove useable by the AufklAbt, even when stationary, since the distances within the battalion are too great. The operational range of the

FuSprech 'a' must be at least doubled. (*)

Ammunition: For the PzSpKp according to KStN 1162, the supply of 2cm and MG ammunition can be reduced by 20 percent. This reduction results from the ever-present shortage of vehicles and weapons. The *Stiel-Handgranate* [stick hand grenade] is not suitable for use in the PzSpWg because of the danger of getting caught when thrown out of the vehicle. In addition, they are cumbersome to carry when leaving the vehicle. We suggest replacing them by *Ei-Handgranate* [egg hand grenade].

In the heavy company, the stock of anti-tank ammunition, mainly the *Panzer-Granatpatrone* [PzGrPtr – cartridge-type armour-piercing shell] can be reduced by 30 percent. A stock of 130 PzGrPtr for each gun, in addition to explosive grenade and PzGr 40, is considered to be sufficient. In contrast, the ammunition stock for the light infantry gun platoon must be increased by 40 percent.

(*) The radios were externally very similar. The early variants of FuSprech 'a' and 'd' had a range of 1km to 3km. The FuSprech 'f', which was introduced from 1942, had a longer range of 5km to 8km. The maximum ranges were achieved with the 2m *Stabantenne* (rod-type antenna), but with the 1.4m version the range was reduced by some 50 percent.

A mixed *Spähtrupp* (reconnaissance section) consisting of an SdKfz 221, a SdKfz 223 and a SdKfz 222. Before mid-1941, only the SdKfz 223 was equipped with a radio.

This SdKfz 263 armoured radio car belonged to PzAufklAbt 57 (6.PzDiv). The crew has applied an effective winter camouflage by using a white lime-based wash. Being a water-soluble coating, it would be removed by the heavy rain of springtime. Note, the snow chains were fitted on the wheels of the first and fourth axles.

Conditions in the east clearly demonstrated the limitations of the German wheeled armoured reconnaissance vehicles. Especially during the *Rasputitsa* (mud season) period, where all type of multi-wheel-drive vehicles skidded off tracks or became bogged down in open terrain often making it impossible to fulfill an important combat reconnaissance mission. A technical or mechanical solution to this problem was possible, but due to the limited capacity and lack of material in German industry this was never accomplished.

On 5 August 1942, a report was delivered by 11.PzDiv:

Field report

Reconnaissance and *Kradschütz:*

The amalgamation of AufklAbt and KradSchtzBtl has been a complete success and the present structure can remain.

KradSchtzKp issued with driven sidecar is considerably inferior to VW-equipped company in terms of off-road capability. The VW *Typ* 82 can only be seen as a temporary solution. The VW *Schwimmwagen* (*Typ* 166) cannot be definitively assessed, since only a few have been delivered. The armoured KradSchtzKp issued with the SdKfz 250 has also proven to be very effective.

All reconnaissance tanks (*) were successfully deployed. But the older-type armoured reconnaissance vehicles (8-Rad) often broke down in the field. The projected PzSpWg *Leopard* and *Luchs* (Lynx) are considered too expensive and also mechanically vulnerable. (**)

Proposal: Installation of an artillery piece on the SdKfz 250. Various items can be built on the chassis of the light (and medium) half-track carrier. This results in a brilliant all-purpose chassis that would also allow type simplification. For the armoured reconnaissance company, allocation of 7.5cm KwK 37 L/24 *Kurzrohr* (*Kurz* – short barrel) some – 33 percent of the total – would be possible. This could be effective for firing high-explosive shells against ground targets or against tanks when using shaped-charge ammunition. The rest of the vehicle could be equipped with 2cm KwK 38 L/55; both types do not require an enclosed turret. The weapon must be fitted with an armoured gun shield (SmK-safe). Also, the fighting compartment must have a folding wire mesh cover to protect the crew from hand grenades and also allow the gun to be used to defend against ground-attack aircraft. (***)

The above type would be the ideal reconnaissance vehicle for all subunits – AufklBatl, KradSchtzBtl, PzGrenRgt and the PzRgt – each would have to be equipped with a platoon of seven cars for reconnaissance or air-defence duties.

(*) Presumably the writer is referring to different variants of the SdKfz 250 and SdKfz 251.

(**) Despite intensive development work, large numbers of standardized *Aufklärungspanzer* (AufKlPz – reconnaissance tank) did not enter service.

(***) This solution would be identical to the weapon system as installed in the SdKfz 222.

This report is also forward-looking, and it can only be assumed that the commander of 11.PzDiv or his senior officers had been aware of similar developments initiated by the HWA. The vehicles mentioned, as well as the proposed reorganization, would be realized (or adapted) for the reconnaissance elements in armoured divisions (see Chapter 8).

In early 1942, an unknown number of SdKfz 221 were modified by mounting 2.8cm s PzB 41 in the turret. The weapon was obsolete at that time and could only be used at short range against a lightly armoured target.

1943 – The Force Grows

8

The year 1942 was to bring fundamental changes for the reconnaissance forces, both technical and organizational.

During 1941 and into 1942, production of armoured reconnaissance vehicles was running at full capacity. But it has been impossible to assemble a sufficiently accurate listing of the equipment issued to the various reconnaissance units.

One of the few reference sources are any existing KStN. But even the evaluation of this information can very difficult, since the actual implementation of these directives in the field cannot be ascertained. Thus, the actual extent of the changes introduced in 1942 is almost impossible to verify.

The commands of the army groups, armies and corps collected reports at ten-day intervals from the units under their command. Unfortunately, these also cannot be used to determine the strengths of the reconnaissance units, since they usually listed only tanks, self-propelled guns, and towed PaK.

The HWA listed in its monthly *Rüststands-Meldungen* (armament status reports) the currently available vehicles, type by type, on all fronts and included those in Germany. But the monthly reports are not very informative, since the armoured reconnaissance vehicles were not clearly listed. However, this was to change slowly with the appointment Heinz Guderian as *Inspekteur der Panzertruppen* (Insp d PzTrp – inspector of armoured forces) in March 1943.

Progress

Operational experience gained between 1939 and 1940 allowed the armoured forces to improve tactical training methods and make improvements to current vehicles, some of which were incorporated on the production line. Specifications for completely new types were issued and German vehicle manufacturers began the design work. Many of the engineers involved were encouraged to

Opposite: In the course of re-arming the PzKpfw IV and StuG in 1942, large numbers of 7.5cm KwK L/24 became available. These weapons were installed as K 37 in the SdKfz 233 and also the SdKfz 251/9. Reconnaissance units and the armoured infantry now had a highly mobile heavy support weapon.

This SdKfz 221 was in service with PzAufklAbt 13 (13.PzDiv) during 1943. Although production of the type ended early in August 1940, existing vehicles continued to be used until the end of hostilities.

carefully evaluate the field reports written during or after the first campaigns before commencing work.

The armament of the SdKfz 221, a 7.92mm MG 34, had proven to be ineffective in battle. Some troops removed the weapon and improvised the installation of a 7.92mm PzB 39. Consequently, production of the SdKfz 221 was cancelled at the end of 1940. The final vehicles were issued to units and a number remained in active service until the end of the war.

As early as the summer of 1941, consideration was being given to mounting the 2.8cm *schwere Panzerbüchse* (s PzB – heavy anti-tank rifle) 41, which had been selected to arm the SdKfz 250/11 armoured half-track. In June 1941, conversion work began on the first 70 SdKfz 221, this included nine vehicles that, at the time, were in service in Libya. The exact number of vehicles converted cannot be verified.

The SdKfz 222 proved to be incomparably better according to available field reports. The 2cm KwK 30 L/55 – the weapon was also installed in the PzKpfw II – proved to be a very versatile heavy machine gun. The high-explosive (HE) ammunition had a devastating effect when firing at artillery and MG emplacements, as well as semi-hard targets. However, the effect against armoured vehicles was limited.

The open-top armour shield (which was explicitly not designated as a turret) gave only limited protection for the crew; they were also exposed to the elements. However, these disadvantages were more than offset by excellent all-round visibility. The open turret also allowed the weapon to have a high range of elevation, making it possible to successfully engage low-flying aircraft.

The desire for heavier weapons was, of course, understandable. Crews of armoured reconnaissance cars were often forced to retreat or knocked out by a better armed opponent. Many were to record their experiences during reconnaissance missions in after-action reports. However, the HWA, as the office responsible for weapon development, was unmovable on its selection of the 2cm cannon (initially KwK 30 L/55 and then KwK 38 L/55) as the armament for the patrols. But, increasingly effective weapons were introduced to equip the heavy companies attached to the patrols for support. To improve their mobility, specialized carrier vehicles (wheeled and half-track) were to be developed and delivered from mid-1942.

The SdKfz 223 (Fu) and the SdKfz 260 (Fu) and also the SdKfz 261 (Fu) were valuable vehicles for the maintenance of radio communications in the face of enemy fire from infantry light weapons and shrapnel.

The use of the heavy SdKfz 231 (8-Rad), SdKfz 232 (8-Rad) and also the SdKfz 263 (8-Rad) was evaluated very differently in the field reports. Many

During 1942, most armoured reconnaissance vehicles were being fitted with radio equipment. This early manufactured SdKfz 231 (now fitted with a *Zerscheller-Platte*) has a 2m rod antenna on the turret, which indicates that the FuSprech 'a' has been replaced by a more powerful FuSprech 'f'.

Above: The final production Büssing-NAG variant was delivered in 1942. The shape of the *Panzeraufbau* (armoured body) was simplified and the front armour increased to 30mm. The *Sternantenne* 'd' indicates that the type carries an 80W Fu 12 and also a FuSprech 'f' short-range radio.

Right: Firepower was increased by mounting the 2cm KwK 38 L/55 in the turret. In theory, this weapon could fire 450 rounds per minute (rpm), whereas the earlier gun was rated at 280rpm.

reconnaissance troop commanders noted that the performance and combat value of these vehicles were almost equivalent to those of the SdKfz 222. But the large vehicle had a very conspicuous profile and often limited cross-country mobility. Also, it was expensive to produce.

As always there were opinions to the contrary. For example, the ability to retreat quickly thanks to the reverse driver was considered positive in many reports. In addition, the more spacious interior allowed the installation of a long-range radio equipment. In the SdKfz 232 (8-Rad), the Fu 12 radio was installed without interfering with combat capability. Three SdKfz 231 (8-Rad) and also three SdKfz 232 (8-Rad) were available in the 1.*schwere* Panzerspäh-Zug (s PzSpZg – [heavy] armoured reconnaissance platoon) of a PzSpKp in accordance with KStN 1162.

Importantly, it must be noted that both SdKfz 221, SdKfz 222 and also the SdKfz 231 (8-Rad) did not carry a transceiver until mid-1941. Radio communications from the reconnaissance squads to the company staff or to other units was ensured by attaching an SdKfz 223. But, this limited availability of radios could delay the transmission of reconnaissance results. Overall, this fact contradicts the general view that all German armoured vehicles were comprehensively equipped with radio. A lot of time passed before the FuSprech 'a' transceiver with its somewhat limited performance (1km range) could be installed in all existing vehicles.

The field reports sent by reconnaissance units assessed the question of off-road mobility very differently. This makes a conclusive and objective

Other changes included a 30mm thick vertical front plate fitted with *Einheits-Sehklappen*, a solid bar-type bumper and shorter front mudguards. A *Zerscheller-Platte* was no longer fitted.

Railway wagons loaded with a delivery, from the manufacturer, of SdKfz 250 Ausf B armoured half-tracks for the PzAufklAbt in PzGrenDiv *Großdeutschland*.

assessment almost impossible since many characteristics are not clearly measurable.

During operations in Poland, more complaints about the lack of off-road capability were reported than during the invasion of France where the majority of roads were hard surfaced. But these experiences were rendered obsolete in the autumn of 1941 in view of the climatic and topographical peculiarities of the Soviet Union. Here German forces were faced with clouds of thick dust in the summer, heavy rain in autumn, snow and ice in winter followed by mud as the spring thaw began. Under these conditions, the deployment of the armoured reconnaissance divisions became somewhat limited. It seemed that the German wheeled armoured reconnaissance vehicles had reached the limits of their capabilities.

Half-tracks

Even before the war began, the introduction of armoured half-track vehicles as armoured reconnaissance vehicles was being considered. Initially rejected for reasons of cost and production capacity, this was now to change.

In 1941, the *leichte gepanzerte Mannschafts-Transportwagen* (le gep MTW – light armoured personnel carrier [SdKfz 250]) reached full production (similar designs, the SdKfz 253 and SdKfz 252, were available as support vehicles for the assault artillery as early as 1940). Initially, it was planned to introduce the SdKfz 250 in parallel with the *mittlere gepanzerte Mannschafts-Transportwagen* (m gep MTW – medium armoured personnel carrier [SdKfz 251]). Officially both were designated *Schützenpanzerwagen* (SPW – armoured infantry carrier) in the rifle units of the *schnellen Truppen* (fast troops) in the Panzer divisions. But the plan had to be dropped, since it was doubtful whether the production of the required numbers would be sufficient to equip entire infantry battalions or regiments.

Now it was decided to use the le gep MTW to reinforce the combat strength of the KradSchtz battalions. Since these units were merged with the reconnaissance battalions within the armoured divisions in 1941/42, these vehicles were soon available for them as well.

The SdKfz 250, like the larger SdKfz 251, was to be introduced in many specialized variants. Some of the non-armoured vehicles and weapons of the heavy company could now be replaced by these armoured half-track vehicles. Also, it would now be possible to establish new smaller units with more effective combat power.

The following variants were assigned to the armoured reconnaissance battalions.

In general, the SdKfz 250 had good off-road mobility. But problems arose due to the vehicle having low ground clearance and also in heavy mud, the running gear become clogged and often failed.

SdKfz 250/1

The basic type carried a crew of six men (driver, co-driver, platoon or half platoon leader, and three gunners.

The vehicle was armed with two MG 34: one could be mounted in the front behind an armoured shield, the other on an anti-aircraft swivel arm that allowed engagement of low-flying aircraft. Some of the vehicles were equipped with the FuSprech 'a' transceiver.

SdKfz 250/3

This variant, a light armoured radio car, carried long-range radio equipment. Three subtypes were introduced of which the AufklAbt received nine SdKfz 250/3 fitted with an 80W Fu 12 and two with a 30W Fu 8. Another SdKfz 250/3, fitted with a Fu 7 (aircraft radio), was issued to the staff of the PzAufklAbt for use by the FliVO.

The complex running gear on the SdKfz 250 placed high demands on the crews and workshop teams. Daily maintenance of all components was essential, costly and necessary. In particular, the rubber pads on the tracks proved to be very vulnerable and were easily lost in action.

Above: In addition to the basic SdKfz 250/1 supplied for a *Halb-Gruppe* (half-group) other variants were available. Two vehicles from 3.PzDiv: the nearest is an SdKfz 250/3 FuWg which was used as a command vehicle; behind is an SdKfz 250/10 armed with a 3.7cm PaK, was issued to the *Zug-Führer* (platoon leader) of the le SchtzKp *gepanzerter* (gp armoured) and also the le AufklKp (gp).

Left: The SdKfz 250/3 could carry variety of radio combinations. The large frame-type antenna was fitted during production was used until the end of 1942. Later vehicles were equipped with a less conspicuous *Sternantenne* 'd'.

SdKfz 250/5

The *leichter Beobachtungs-Panzerwagen* (le BeobPzWg – light armoured observation vehicle) was a specialized type issued to the PzSpKp 'c' (KStN 1162c) from 1942. Although similar to the SdKfz 250/3, this variant was equipped with an 80 W Fu 12 radio. The armament consisted of a MG 34 machine gun, as well as a 7.92mm MP.

All SdKfz 250/1, SdKfz 250/3 and SdKfz 250/5 were initially equipped with the FuSprech 'a' transceiver. In June 1943, this radio (range 1km) was replaced by the more powerful FuSprech 'f' (range 6km to 8km).

At around the same time, the *Panzeraufbau* on the type was re-designed to simplify production. It would now be fabricated from a smaller number of armour plates, and also fewer complex shaped parts. This variant was designated Ausf B, the original version became Ausf A. At aroud the same time, the MG 34 was replaced by the MG 42.

Improved Firepower

Experiences in Russia as well as in North Africa led to demands to equip the reconnaissance elements in the tank divisions with effective support weapons.

Despite its small calibre, the 2cm KwK 30 L/55 had proven to be very effective as a heavy machine gun. During 1942, it was to be replaced in the SdKfz 222 and SdKfz 232 by the improved 2cm KwK 38 L/55. From the end of 1942, this even more effective weapon was also to be mounted in the SdKfz 250.

SdKfz 250/9

In order to give the PzAufklKp equipped with armoured half-tracks as much firepower as possible, it was decided to mount the 2cm KwK 38L/55 as used in the SdKfz 222 on the SdKfz 250.

Initially, the complete gun assembly and pedestal mounting were installed unchanged in the SdKfz 250 Ausf A. But on the SdKfz 250 Ausf B, the simplified superstructure allowed a new space-saving *Hängelafette* (suspended gun mount) to be used and also enabled engineers to utilize and modify the original SdKfz 222 turret, which was also rotatable.

SdKfz 250/10

In order to provide the *leichte Schützen-Kompanien* (*gepanzert*) (le SchtzKp [gp] – light rifle companies [armoured]) to KStN 1113 [gp] with increased firepower, platoon leaders were assigned the SdKfz 250/10. This vehicle carried the 3.7cm PaK in place of the MG 34. The gunner was protected by a small shield.

Opposite: The radio equipment in an SdKfz 250/3 was installed in a large rack, which left little space for the four-man crew and their personal kit. The operator in the black uniform wears a *Blitz* (lightning bolt) badge of the intelligence troops.

Above: The first prototypes of the SdKfz 250/9, were built on a Demag D7p chassis with bodywork fabricated from mild steel sheet. Many details, such as the position of the exhaust system, differed to series production SdKfz 250 armoured half-tracks.

Right: The 2cm KwK 38 L/55 on a *Sockellafette* could be installed in both the SdKfz 222 and SdKfz 250/9 without any major problems.

Left: A poorly camouflaged SdKfz 250/9 positioned at the edge of a small wood. The 2cm KwK 38 L/55 had a high rate of fire which made the weapon very effective against low-flying aircraft.

Below: An SdKfz 250/9 of the PzAufklAbt in 2.PzDiv. The crew has placed a fitted waterproof cover over the turret to protect the weapons and keep the interior dry.

Above: At the beginning of 1942, the AufklAbt (mot) and the KradSchtzBtl were successively merged to form the PzAufklAbt, which significantly increased combat strength. The platoon leaders in light rifle companies were issued with the SdKfz 250/10. The vehicle is in service with 1.SS-PzDiv LAH.

Right: Vehicles of the PzAufklAbt of PzGrenDiv GD, concealed from the enemy observers in a *Balka* (shallow depression). The vehicle on the left is an SdKfz 250/10.

This vehicle was also available to the *leichten Aufklärungs-Kompanien* (*gepanzert*) (le AufklKp [gp] – light reconnaissance companies [armoured]) of the PzAufklAbt. Since the le AufklKp (gp) was identical to the le SchtzKp (gp), both were issued in accordance to KStN 1113 (gp).

SdKfz 250/7

This variant carried an 8cm GrW 34 heavy mortar and team. The weapon was mounted inside the vehicle, but could be dismounted and fired using a base plate carried on the rear of the vehicle. The SdKfz 250/7 could carry 66 mortar rounds and was armed with either an MG 34 or MG 42 for self-defence. This vehicle was also assigned to le AufklKp (gp) as detailed in KStN 1113 (gp).

7.5cm le IG 18

The 7.5cm le IG 18 had proven its usefulness time and again in the heavy companies of the PzAufklAbt, when deployed to provide effective supporting fire in an attack or in defence. This effectiveness, however, was diminished by the fact that it was generally towed by a soft-skinned vehicle.

In 1942, efforts began to improve both mobility and armour protection of the weapon.

In 1942, the heavy 8cm GrW 34 was installed in both the SdKfz 250 and SdKfz 251 armoured personnel carriers. The heavy platoons in light infantry companies were issued with the SdKfz 250/7 or the SdKfz 251/2 which boosted the combat value of the PzAufklAbt. The weapon could also be dismounted when required.

SdKfz 233

Since large stocks of redundant 7.5cm *Sturmkannone* (StuK – assault gun) L/24 were still available in 1942, a number were re-designated as the 7.5cm KwK 37 L/24 and fitted with a special mounting for installation in the armoured superstructure of 8-Rad vehicles. (This weapon was also mounted in the medium armoured half-track designated SdKfz 251/9.)

Initially, PzFuWg (SdKfz 263), drawn from maintenance facilities in the Reich, were used for this conversion. A total of 32 rounds of 7.5cm ammunition were stowed inside the vehicle designated as the SdKfz 233. A single 7.92mm MG 34 was mounted for self-defence.

SdKfz 250/8

Since the 7.5cm-armed SdKfz 233 proved to be very effective in service, it became obvious to military planners that the SdKfz 250 could be similarly armed and issued to rifle and reconnaissance companies.

From the end of 1943, an improved variant of the 7.5cm KwK 37 L/24 became available; the 7.5cm K 51 L/24. This version did not require a pedestal mounting, and so could be easily fitted, without time-consuming conversion work, in the superstructure of the light armoured half-track carrier. By the end of the war, a total of 60 SdKfz 250 Ausf B had

Opposite top: Büssing-NAG delivered the final version of their *Typ GS* heavy (SdKfz 231) armoured car in 1942. On the front of the vehicle, to the right of the driving lamp light, are a number of smoke grenades were attached.

Opposite bottom: Large numbers early production SdKfz 231 continued to be used by front-line units, and many survived for a surprisingly long time.

Below: Spring 1943: The leading SdKfz 231, in this reconnaissance squad from 14.PzDiv, has been simply camouflaged under bundles of reeds.

Above: An early SdKfz 232 (8-Rad) has been repainted as part of a programme, initiated in early 1943, to the change from *dunkelgrau* (dark grey) to *dunkelgelb* (dark yellow).

Right: A late production SdKfz 231 in service with 1.Kp of PzAufklAbt 13 (13.PzDiv) passes a loaded *Maultier* (mule) half-track truck. The elaborately camouflaged vehicle carries petrol canisters to extend the range of a reconnaissance patrol.

been completed and designated SdKfz 250/8. In the long term, these vehicles were to replace the SdKfz 250/10 armed with 3.7cm PaK, but this was never achieved.

A New Armoured Scout Car

As early as 1940, *Waffenprüfamter* (Wa Prüf – weapons testing department) 6 of the HWA issued orders for the design and development of a new type of armoured reconnaissance vehicle. The specification called for an eight-wheel vehicle, similar to the eight-wheeled SdKfz 231, SdKfz 232 and SdKfz 233, but with improved key mechanical and structural details. The new type was to use unitary construction (no separate chassis) fabricated from armour plate which was 30mm frontal at the front. In a departure from German practice, the type was to be diesel powered.

By the end of 1943, both Büssing-NAG and Tatra had designed and begun development trials a new armoured reconnaissance vehicle under the designation *Achtradwagen Tropen* (Tp – Tropical) (8-Rad [Tp] – eight-wheeled vehicle [tropical] originally intended for use in hot and humid regions. Although it was clear that the main armament would be the 2cm KwK 38 L/55 in a *Hängelafette* another variant had already been developed.

The 7.5cm K 37 was installed to the right of the driver which severely limited traverse (21 degrees). The vehicle now carried a crew of three, since the rear driving position was not installed. The vehicle, produced in 1942, has been painted in two-colour tropical camouflage (grey-green blotches over a sand yellow).

Above: Development work on an improved PzSpWg (8-Rad) had been initiated in 1940 and was completed in 1942. The 8-Rad [Tp] was similar in appearance to its predecessor, but had an armoured hull, and larger wheels. This pre-production model is fitted with a SdKfz 231 turret.

Right: The vehicle had a much-improved off-road capability, better ground clearance and wading depth. The 8-Rad (Tp) was fitted with a V-12 Tatra 103 diesel engine.

Above: The first production model, the SdKfz 234/1, mounted a 2cm KwK 38 L/55 and a 7.92mm MG 42 in an open multi-faced turret. The second variant (above), designated SdKfz 234/2, mounted a 5cm KwK 39/1 L/60 and a 7.92mm MG 42 in an oval-shaped turret.

Left: From 1943, the SdKfz 234/2, now known as the *'Puma'*, began to be fitted with an NKAV (smoke grenade dispenser) mounted on each side of the turret.

SdKfz 234

The new heavy armoured scout car went into production in December 1943. The armoured body strongly resembled the eight-wheeled Type GS (SdKfz 231). A large well-shaped revolving turret was mounted on the superstructure, and carried a 5cm KwK 39/1 L/60 with a coaxial 7.92mm MG 34. All SdKfz 234 were equipped with the FuSprech 'f' transceiver. Every second vehicle was additionally equipped with a long-range 80W Fu 12. The vehicles were organized according to KStN 1162a (PzSpKp 'a'), with 25 vehicles assigned to each company. After production of 100 SdKfz 234 the production was changed to the 2cm KwK 38 L/55 in a *Hängelafette*, the variant armed with the 5cm KwK L/60 was redesignated SdKfz 234/2.

SdKfz 234/1

When the SdKfz 234 was discontinued, the SdKfz 234/1 armed with a 2cm KwK 38 L/55 mounted on a *Hängelfafette* in an open-top turret entered

production. It was issued in accordance to a specifically written KStN 1162d (PzSpKp 'd') which showed that each company was to receive 25 vehicles. The radio fit was identical to that of the SdKfz 234. Some 230 of the SdKfz 234/1 had been delivered by various manufacturers by the time the war ended in May 1945 the end of the war.

SdKfz 234/3

Due to the obvious successes of the *Kanonenwagen*, a variant of the 8-Rad (Tp) was to be equipped with a 7.5cm K L/24, as mounted in the production SdKfz 251/19 and also the SdKfz 250/8. Initially, the SdKfz 234/1 and SdKfz 234/3 were built in identical numbers, underlining the combat value of these well-armed and highly mobile assault guns. But records show that more of the 2cm-armed SdKfz 234/1 had been built by the end of the war. The SdKfz 234/3 carried only a single FuSprech 'f' transceiver.

February 1943: Camouflaged with white-wash paint, reconnaissance vehicles from the PzAufklAbt in 2.S-PzDiv *Das Reich* SS-Pz advance through a battle-scarred town during the fighting to recapture Kharkov. The column is led by an SdKfz 247 Ausf B, followed by an SdKfz 263 and an SdKfz 260 of the *Nachrichtung-Zug* (NachrZg – signals platoon).

Above: In July 1942, Büssing-NAG began production of an improved variant of the *Typ* GS (8-Rad). The vehicle was armed with the more effective 2cm KwK 38 L/55 and the thickness of front plates on the turret and superstructure was increased from 14.5mm to 30mm.

Right: In 1943, the large and conspicuous frame-type antenna fitted on the SdKfz 232 began to be replaced by a *Sternantenne* 'd'.

Left: The 7.5cm K 37-armed SdKfz 233, known as the *'Kanonenwagen'*, provided the PzAufklAbt with formidable firepower. But the *Sockellafette* took up a lot of space, leaving barely enough any room for the driver.

Below: This late production SdKfz 233 has additional armour plates fitted to the top of the fighting compartment to improve protection. The crew has stowed boxes containing K 37 ammunition on the engine deck.

A small series of armoured reconnaissance vehicles, based on the proven PzKpfw 38(t) chassis, was produced at the end of 1943. The superstructure was fabricated from riveted armour plate and it was armed with a 2cm KwK 38 L/55 and 7.92mm MG 42 fitted on space-saving *Hängelafette*. The *Sternantenne* 'd' indicates that the vehicle is fitted with the long-range Fu 12.

Reconnaissance Tanks

Germany only began the development of a new type of light tank late in the war. It is important to understand that the term *leichter Panzer* (light tank) here does not necessarily describe combat vehicles of light weight or small size. The classic light tank after 1940 was defined by the fact that its design made it capable of tasks different from those of the main battle tanks.

Neither the PzKpfw I, developed in 1933, nor the PzKpfw II introduced around 1936 could meet such requirements. The PzKpfw I initially served to rapidly build up large armoured formations and later for training thousands of tank crews. These vehicles were also used to trial of operational principles in large-scale manoeuvres.

The PzKpfw II, was introduced as an expedient in 1941. This was due long delays in the production of the PzKpfw III and also the PzKpfw IV main battle tanks, which meant wartime requirements could not be met. Unfortunately, the majority PaKpfw II had been in service since 1935 and worn out mechanically and outdated in combat terms.

Even before the outbreak of war, various tank projects, some of them very different, were to be initiated. Neither the *Versuchs-Kampfwagen* (VK – prototype armoured vehicle) 601 nor the VK 1801 (the PzKpfw I *neue Ausfuhrung* [nA – new type]) or PzKpfw I nA *verstärkt* (verst – reinforced [heavier] armour) were to be introduced in large numbers. The PzKpfw II Ausf G and PzKpfw II nA (verst) followed, but were also built in only small numbers. Most of these vehicles served with police units. Construction wise, all of these tank types were independent developments that did not use any significant components of the earlier PzKpfw I and PzKpfw II.

SdKfz 123 *Luchs*

In 1941, another model was developed to production readiness, the VK 1303. Designated PzKpfw II Ausf L, this light tracked vehicle began to be built in mid-1942. Initially it was planned to produce 800, a surprisingly high number. The type did not resemble the pre-war variants of the PzKpfw II.

The vehicle mounted a 2cm KwK 38 L/55 with a coaxial MG, since it was

The advantages of using a *Hängelafette* are obvious. The same type of mounting was installed in the SdKfz 250/9 Ausf B and also the 8-Rad (Tp).

Above: The PzKpfw II Ausf L, commonly called *'Luchs'*, was ready for production in 1941. Although the official designation refers to PzKpfw II 'family' of tanks, the chassis (with torsion bar suspension), superstructure and turret were completely new.

Right: Although originally designed to be a fast and highly manoeuvrable reconnaissance vehicle, the PzKpfw II Ausf L *'Luchs'* had 30mm frontal armour. This tank of 4.PzDiv was modified in the field by adding an additional amour plate.

planned as a fast reconnaissance vehicle. Mechanically it was impressive, being powered by a 6,750cc Maybach HL 66P 180hp water-cooled engine which gave the type an excellent power-to-weight ratio and a top speed of 60kph. The vehicle was fitted with *Schactellaufwerk* (interleaved [over lapping]) disc wheels, torsion bar suspension with wide tracks which gave the type excellent off-road mobility even in mud and snow.

The AufklPz was equipped with an 80W Fu 12 radio and a FuSprech 'f'. Production was discontinued after just 100 had been completed, although at the time there were a number of prototypes with sloped armour undergoing trials. Also, a variant armed with a 5cm PaK 38 had been designed. This decision to cancel the SdKfz 123 was probably made because more powerful reconnaissance tanks were planned using PzKpfw V *Panther* components. But even these proposals did not get beyond the drawing board stage.

A new KStN, the 1162b, was to be made for the *Luchs*. The vehicles were assigned to two units, with 25 tanks each going to 2./PzAufklAbt 9 (9.PzDiv) and 2./PzAufklAbt 4 (4.PzDiv).

SdKfz 140/1

Bôhmische-Mährische Maschinenfabrik (BMM), the manufacturer of the PzKpfw 38(t), was issued with a contract to develop a reconnaissance tank in October 1943, and the company was ordered to utilize many of the

In typical Panzer fashion the crew has placed spare track links on the glacis plate to gain additional protection. The curved items, placed above the visors on the front plate, are spare rim segments which fitted on the solid running wheels.

Generators were available to produce electricity to power radios when reconnaissance vehicles were operating from a stationary position. The *Maschinensatz* (machine set) GG 400 unit, known as the '*Tiger Würfel*', was a two-stroke engine-powered portable generator which could produce up to 400W of power.

components used on the original tank. The type had a riveted superstructure fitted with a modified turret mounting a 2cm KwK 38 L/55 in a *Hängelafette*. Military planners decided to issue a production order for only 70 of the type. The tanks were issued according to KStN 1162, but most were assigned to only two units: 2./PzAufklAbt *Großdeutschland* (PzGrenDiv GD) and 1./PzAufklAbt 3 (3.PzDiv).

Cross-country Vehicles

By 1941, large parts of the German army were equipped with motor vehicles that had been developed before the outbreak of war.

Particularly on the East Front, civilian motor vehicles and even basically militarized types were to prove completely unsuitable; the adverse conditions on the battlefront resulted in a vast number of mechanical breakdowns.

The *leichte* (le – light) and *mittlere* (m – medium) *geländegängige Personenkraftwagen* (gl Pkw – cross-country passenger car) manufactured by Stöwer and Horch were complex all-wheel-drive vehicles. Although these were certainly powerful, they proved to be mechanically too complicated and consequently, totally unsuitable for the requirements of the war in the east. In

addition, the complexity and the associated high production costs were totally opposite to the economic production of large quantities.

With the introduction of the war economy, production of a new off-road vehicle began. This was based on the KdF-Wagen – a light car designed to allow large numbers of the German population access to inexpensive mobility – had been developed in 1936. The HWA specified that the vehicle was to have open bodywork, and a maximum weight of less than 1,000kg (including three men and equipment). Mass production was to be possible in high numbers at low manufacturing costs.

The *Typ* 82 *Kübelwagen* was powered by a four-cylinder air-cooled petrol engine and, for simplicity and ease of maintenance, two-wheel drive. The low weight, combined with high ground clearance, resulted in outstanding manoeuvrability even over the most difficult terrain. More than 50,000 of the type had been produced by the end of the war – by comparison, more than 500,000 Jeeps were produced for the US military.

The *Typ* 87 *Kommandeurwagen* (command car) was a sub-type of little consequence which utilized the same engine and basic chassis. In essence it was a four-wheel-drive saloon car (VW Beetle) of which only 500 were produced.

The PzKpfw II Ausf L *Luchs*, had a robust torsion bar suspension and the running gear was an improvement on that used on the pre-war PzKpfw II. The wider tracks and interleaved disc-type road wheels helped to prevent mud from clogging the running gear.

Above: Adolf Hitler and a number of senior officers inspect a pre-production VW *Typ* 166 *Schwimmwagen*. The amphibious vehicle, initially called *Kradschützen-Wagen*, was used primarily for reconnaissance purposes.

Right: With the VW *Typ* 82 *Kübelwagen*, the German armed forces were finally to receive a standardized passenger car that was economical to produce. Despite the lack of all-wheel drive, the vehicles had legendary off-road performance.

Left: The air-cooled engine in the *Kübelwagen* was mounted in the rear of the vehicle and was easily accessible for maintenance.

Below: The *Typ* 82 was a simple, almost spartanly equipped vehicle. A canvas folding top, with insertable side screens, protected the crew from the weather.

Above: Production of the Büssing-NAG *Typ* GS (8-Rad) continued until November 1943, with an average of 25 vehicles being built every month. In 1943, the front-line inventory of these vehicles fluctuated between 300 and 400 vehicles.

Right: Engineers remove the engine cooling-fan assembly from an 8-Rad. The radiator was positioned ahead of the rear-mounted engine, to prevent it from being damaged.

By 1942, VW had developed an amphibious off-road vehicle from the *Typ* 82, which was to go into production as the *Typ* 166 *Schwimmwagen*. The vehicle was fitted with the same type of air-cooled engine principle, as the *Typ* 82 or *Typ* 87, but with power slightly increased to 25hp. It was also fitted with a new type selectable all-wheel drive and an ultra-low gear for cross-country mobility. The performance of this car was legendary. Some 14,000 vehicles were produced at the VW factory in Wolfsburg, until Allied bombers struck and destroyed the facilities.

Both the *Kübelwagen* and the *Schwimmwagen* were intended to supplement or replace the powered sidecars in service with the rifle units.

Organizational Changes

Amalgamation

Before the start of *Fall Blau* (Plan Blue), the attack on the Caucasus in the summer of 1942, the general merging of the reconnaissance detachments and KradSchtz battalions of the PzDiv and InfDiv (mot) took place. The *Panzerspäh-Schwadronen* (PzSpSchw – armoured car squadrons) were transferred to the KradSchtzBtl as the 1.PzSpKp. The KradSchtz squadrons were also partially transferred. All other squadrons were disbanded. The traditional designation *Schwadron* was now replaced by *Kompanie* (an exception remained the 24.PzDiv [this was a traditional unit formed from the 1.KavDiv] which was raised in December 1941).

Infantry Divisions

The equipment of the reconnaissance elements in the conventional infantry divisions varied widely.

Some of the divisions had a motorized *schnelle Abteilung* (rapid battalion), where the *Panzer-Jäger-Kompanien* (PzJgKp – tank destroyer companies) tank destroyer companies were reinforced with a *Radfahr-Schwadron* (bicycle squadron). The composition of these mobile units differed greatly, the number of PzJgKp varied from one to three and the same was true for the wheeled squadrons.

Few 'normal' InfDiv had capable reconnaissance elements. The 22.InfDiv had a reconnaissance detachment with a PzAufklKp (PzSpWg [8-Rad] in accordance with KStN 1162), reinforced by a platoon with six SdKfz 233 according to KStN 1138. In addition, there were three KradSchtzKp and a heavy company. This corresponded approximately to the reconnaissance strength of a PzDiv as being 1941 or an InfDiv (mot).

An SdKfz 250/3 (FuWg) fitted with a *Sternantenne* 'd' leads a column of armoured personnel carriers from a PzAufklAbt.

The following organizational tables, for reconnaissance elements in various major German units in June 1942, show some contradictions.

InfDiv (mot)

The ten available infantry divisions (mot) were fully motorized and some also had a tank battalion. The reconnaissance elements were virtually equivalent to those of the 22.InfDiv (see above), but did not have a 'Kanonen-Zug' with six SdKfz 233.

Opposite: The commander of KradSchtzAbt GD in his SdKfz 247 Ausf B armoured command vehicle. The large star-type aerial indicates that it has been fitted with an Fu 12 long-range radio.

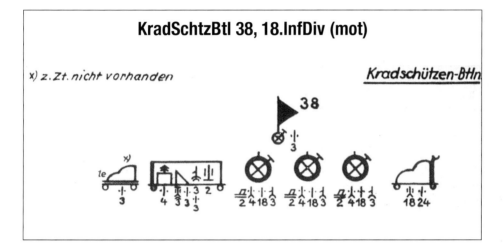

InfDiv *Großdeutschland*

Although established as an infantry division, this elite unit had two strong infantry regiments, a tank battalion and an assault gun (StuG) battalion, in addition to several subunits.

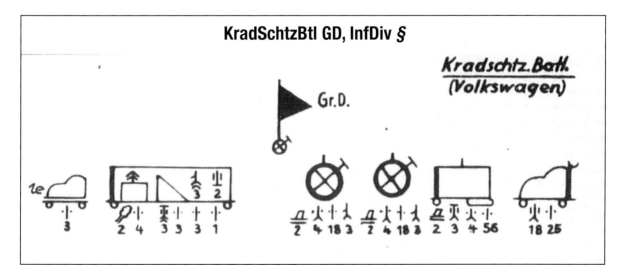

Above: In 1942, increasing numbers of reconnaissance units were being equipped with VW *Kübelwagen* and *Schwimmwagen*, but a large number of *Beiwagen-Kräder* were to remain in service until the end of the war.

Right: In an emergency, the two-man machine gun team could easily recover their relatively light motorcycle combination.

The KradSchtzAbt was merged with the AufklAbt, and thus had a PzSpKp formed as detail in KStN 1162, a le SchtzKp (gp) as shown in KStN 1113 (gp), two KradSchtzKp, a heavy company and a supply train. Both KradSchtz companies were equipped with cross-country cars, but It is not known whether these were the *Kübelwagen* or *Schwimmwagen*.

SS-Div (mot) *Wiking*

This *Waffen*-SS unit was equipped almost the same as an InfDiv (mot), but the KradSchtzBtl was still separate from the reconnaissance division.

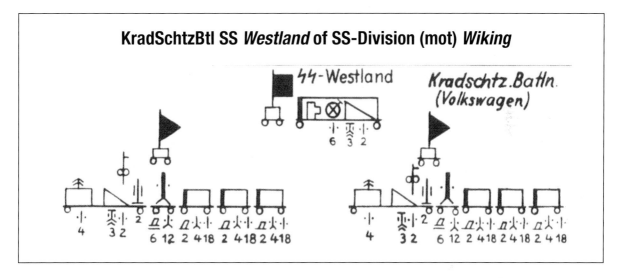

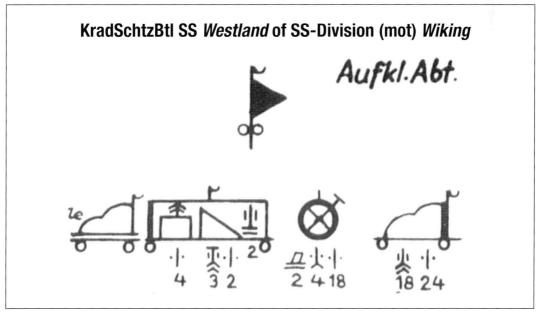

SS-KavDiv

The SS-KavDiv had only rudimentary reconnaissance elements with two wheeled squadrons (reconnaissance) and one heavy company.

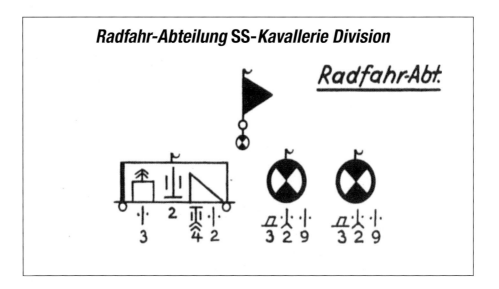

6.PzDiv

The reconnaissance elements in 6.PzDiv were integrated with the KradSchtzAbt. KradSchtzAbt 6 had a PzSpKp in accordance with KStN 1162, a le SchtzKp (gp) to table KStN 1113 (gp), and two KradSchtzKp, a heavy company and a light column. Both KradSchtzKp were equipped with cross-country vehicles. But, once again, it is not known whether these were *Typ* 82 or *Typ* 166.

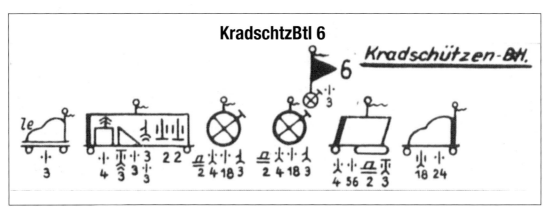

8.PzDiv

The KradSchtzBtl 8 (8.PzDiv) corresponded to that in 6.PzDiv, but with one difference that le SchtzKp (gp) – was yet to be assigned.

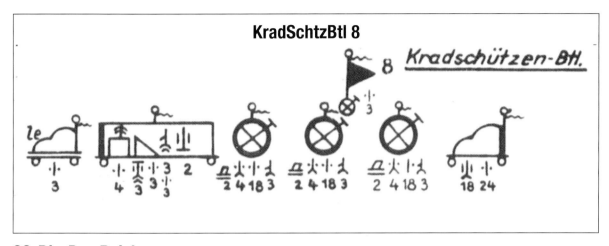

KradSchtzBtl 8

SS-Div *Das Reich*

In the summer of 1942, the SS-*Division Das Reich* was approximately equivalent to the InfDiv *Großdeutschland*. The KradSchtzAbt was merged with the AufklAbt, and thus had one PzSpKp to table KStN 1162, one le SchtzKp (gp) in accordance with KStN 1113 (gp), also two KradSchtzKp, a heavy company and a supply train. Both KradSchtz companies were equipped cross-country vehicles. Again, the type of cannot be determined, but it is most probable that both the *Typ* 82 and *Typ* 166 were issued. In 1943, the unit was to be converted, firstly, into a PzGrenDiv, and then a Panzer Division.

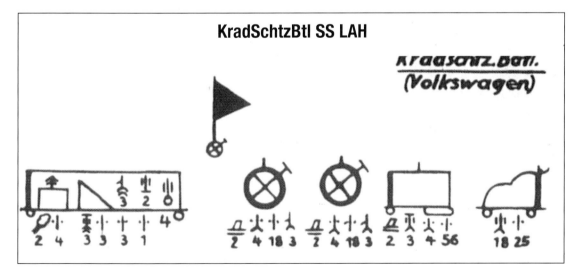

KradSchtzBtl SS LAH

Basic Structures

Based on the experience gained in the first campaigns of the war, the organizational structures were adapted to several times depending requirements.

The PzAufklAbt of 1942 consisted mainly of the following subunits:

PzSpKp

By 1943, the PzSpKp formed in accordance to KStN 1162, was to be the most important component of the PzAufklAbt.

Since production of the SdKfz 221 ceased at the end of 1940, KStN 1162 (PzSpKp) was to be updated in November 1941. This also fulfilled the desire for better armament, as the number of light armoured cars was increased to 12. Also, instead of four SdKfz 223 (Fu), six were now available. It can be assumed that newly assigned armoured scout cars were equipped with FuSprech 'a' transceiver. Existing vehicles were converted by the workshop services as part of ordered organizational changes, always depending on the material situation and conditions on the frontline.

The problem in this arrangement was that the targeted supply of SdKfz 222 could also be met by deliveries of SdKfz 221 from old stocks or from repair facilities in Germany. Also, the residual parts of exhausted divisions

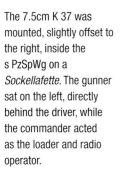

The 7.5cm K 37 was mounted, slightly offset to the right, inside the s PzSpWg on a *Sockellafette*. The gunner sat on the left, directly behind the driver, while the commander acted as the loader and radio operator.

Panzerspäh-Kompanie
according to KStN 1162 dated 1 November 1941

Kompanietrupp

1. (schwerer) Zug

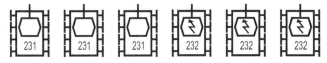

2. (leichter) Zug

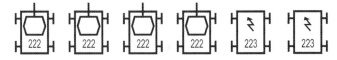

3. (leichter) Zug

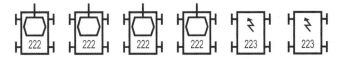

4. (leichter) Zug

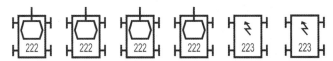

Kfz Inst *Gruppe*   **Gepäcktross**

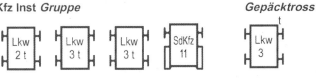

Gefechts-Tross

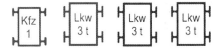

Type of soft-skinned vehicle depended on availability and theatre of war. SdKfz 222 could be substituted by SdKfz 221.

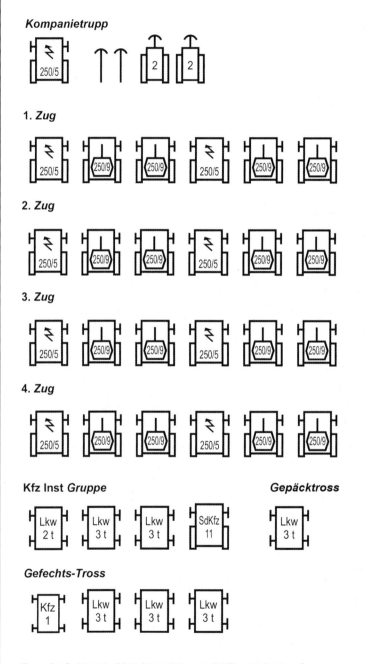

Panzerspäh-Kompanie 'c'
according to KStN 1162 (c) dated 5 February 1943

Kompanietrupp

1. Zug

2. Zug

3. Zug

4. Zug

Kfz Inst *Gruppe*

Gepäcktross

Gefechts-Tross

Type of soft-skinned vehicle depended on availability and theatre of war. SdKfz 2 *Kettenkrad* could be substituted by *Beiwagen-Krad*.

transferred to the Reich for rest and refurbishment were often distributed to other front-line units. Thus, this measure could only be implemented gradually. The PzSpKp according to KStN 1162 was not subject to any further significant changes before the end of the war. The number of *Kradmelder* (dispatch rider) and also of cars and trucks was to be reduced with each update.

PzSpKp 'c'

With the availability of the SdKfz 250/9, the formation of a new very powerful subunit for the PzAufklAbt, the PzSpKp 'c' to table KStN 1162(c), began at the end of 1943. A total of 16 of these vehicles, together with eight SdKfz 250/5, formed eight reconnaissance squads. Every second SdKfz 250/9 was equipped with a FuSprech 'f' transceiver. Each SdKfz 250/5 carried a long-range 80W radio (Fu 12).

A *Kradmelder*, whose distinctive long leather coat was his only protection from the freezing cold or torrential rain. The motorcycle, here a DKW NZ 500, was to remain irreplaceable for fast liaison duties on all battlefronts until the war ended.

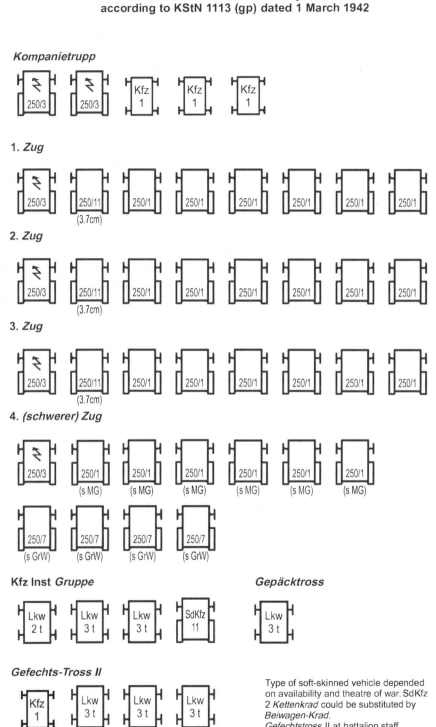

leichte Schützen-Kompanie
according to KStN 1113 (gp) dated 1 March 1942

Kompanietrupp

250/3 | 250/3 | Kfz 1 | Kfz 1 | Kfz 1

1. Zug

250/3 | 250/11 (3.7cm) | 250/1 | 250/1 | 250/1 | 250/1 | 250/1 | 250/1

2. Zug

250/3 | 250/11 (3.7cm) | 250/1 | 250/1 | 250/1 | 250/1 | 250/1 | 250/1

3. Zug

250/3 | 250/11 (3.7cm) | 250/1 | 250/1 | 250/1 | 250/1 | 250/1 | 250/1

4. (schwerer) Zug

250/3 | 250/1 (s MG) | 250/1 (s MG) | 250/1 (s MG) | 250/1 (s MG) | 250/1 (s MG) | 250/1 (s MG)

250/7 (s GrW) | 250/7 (s GrW) | 250/7 (s GrW) | 250/7 (s GrW)

Kfz Inst Gruppe

Lkw 2 t | Lkw 3 t | Lkw 3 t | SdKfz 11

Gepäcktross

Lkw 3 t

Gefechts-Tross II

Kfz 1 | Lkw 3 t | Lkw 3 t | Lkw 3 t

Type of soft-skinned vehicle depended on availability and theatre of war. SdKfz 2 *Kettenkrad* could be substituted by *Beiwagen-Krad*.
Gefechtstross II at battalion staff.

Elements of the PzAufklAbt in SS-PzDiv LAH during the recapture of Kharkov in spring 1943. The SdKfz 263 (left) is fitted with additional armour, but the conspicuous frame-type antenna has been removed and replaced with a 2.8m *Stabantenne*, which indicates that the vehicle carries a portable Torn FuG transceiver.

Light Rifle Company (armoured)

When the SdKfz 250 light armoured personnel carrier became available, the majority were assigned to the rifle battalions, and issued to their le SchtzKp (gp) in accordance with KStN 1113 (gp).

This company now had 31 light armoured personnel carriers which made it a more effective fighting unit than its predecessor, which had been equipped with motorcycles.

The riflemen could now bring their weapons to the enemy under light armour protection. Each of the three platoons was issued with seven MG 34 machine guns and a 3.7cm PaK-armed SdKfz 250/10. The heavy platoon was equipped with two 8cm GrW 34-armed SdKfz 250/7.

The next update of KStN 1113 (gp), was valid for both a light rifle company and a light armoured reconnaissance company. The name change occurred at around the same time as the renaming of the rifle battalions to PzAufklAbt in 1943.

KradSchtzKp 'b'

Since not all rifle battalions could be immediately equipped with light rifle companies, the KradSchtzKp continued to be used (KStN 1112). The unit had some 60 heavy motorcycles with sidecars. Heavy infantry weapons included 18 heavy MG 34 and two 8cm s GrW 34.

le SchtzKp (mot) on Volkswagen

The le SchtzKp (mot) on Volkswagen detailed in KStN 1113, was to gradually supplement or replace KradSchtzKp 'b'. The organizational layout corresponded more or less to that of this company. Instead of powered sidecars, 51 Volkswagens, possibly a mixture of *Typ* 82 and *Typ* 166, were assigned with other vehicles to the company.

Heavy Company

This was formed as of individual *Teileinheit* (TE – sub units) and were intended to provide support in all combat situations.

(TE) *Führer schwere Kompanie* to KStN 1121.
(TE) *Geschütz-Zug* with two 7.5cm le IG 18 (mot Zug) to KStN 1123.
(TE) *Panzerjäger-Zug* with three 5cm PaK 38 (mot Zug) to KStN 1122a.
(TE) *Panzerjäger-Gruppe* (PzJgGrp – anti-tank group) with three 2.8cm s PzB 41(mot Zug) to KStN 1127.
(TE) *Pionier-Zug* (mot).

Opposite: To preserve valuable equipment, particularly wheeled vehicles (here a platoon of SdKfz 233), all would be loaded on railway wagons for transportation to the battlefront.

Below: Whenever possible reconnaissance units would attempt to capture enemy soldiers. Here a Russian infantryman awaits interrogation by a German intelligence officer.

Above: In November 1942, SS-PzDiv LAH was based at Montauban, in Vichy (southern) France. Here elements of their PzAufklAbt assemble for a parade; on the right are two SdKfz 223, with an SdKfz 261 to the left.

Right: This SdKfz 251/1 has, in addition to division marking, been painted with the distinctive sword-waving ghost symbol used by 11.PzDiv. The vehicle is in service with 2.KradSchtzKp (61. KradSchtzAbt).

Above: Unit commanders attend a pre-battle briefing alongside a SdKfz 232.In the background, tanks of 9.PzDiv form up, for the attack.

Left: Spring 1942: This SdKfz 263 armoured radio car is in service with the KradSchtzAbt of 7.PzDiv.

A heavily damaged SdKfz 232 (8-Rad) from the PzAufklAbt 19 (19. PzDiv). For operations on the Kursk salient, all German units involved received special markings; here two white vertical bars identify the division. The Red Army troops are riding on a British-built Infantry Tank Mk IV Churchill, one of the many supplied during World War II.

(Note, the *Panzerjäger-Gruppe* with three 2.8cm s PzB 41 could not be assigned to all rifle battalions. Some units received two tank destroyer platoons.)

In March 1943, the heavy company was significantly reinforced.

(TE) *Führer schwere Kompanie* (gp) to KStN 1121a (gp).
(TE) *Geschütz-Zug* with two 7.5cm le IG 18 (SdKfz 251/4) to KStN 1123a (gp).
(TE) *Panzerjäger-Zug* with three 7.5cm PaK 40 L/48 (SdKfz 251/4) to KStN 1145 (gp).
(TE) *schwerer Kanonen-Zug* (7.5cm) (SdKfz 251/9) to KStN 1125 (gp).
OR
(TE) *schwerer Panzerspäh-Zug* 7.5cm (SdKfz 233) to KStN 1138.
(TE) *Pionier-Zug* 'a' (gp) to KStN 1124a (gp).

(Note, the gun platoon of two 7.5cm le IG 18 were towed by SdKfz 251/4. Depending on the type of unit, either a platoon of six SdKfz 233 or SdKfz 251/9 was attached. The engineer platoon 'a' (gp) was equipped with six SdKfz 251/7.)

Below: An SdKfz 247 Ausf B armoured command vehicle in service with PzAufklAbt 6 (6.PzDiv) during the battle for the Kursk salient. The division sign (very similar to that of 2.SS-PzDiv *Das Reich*) used by the unit during the operation is visible on the side of the superstructure. Originally the type was not fitted with radio equipment, but this was rectified as the war progressed.

Schwere Kompanie
consisting of subunits, example PzAufklAbt 24, 24.PzDiv, 1943

Führer schwere Kompanie (gp) KStN 1121 a (gp)

Kfz *Inst Gruppe*

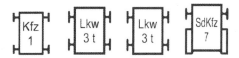

Gefechts-Tross   ***Gepäcktross***

Geschütz-Zug with two 7.5cm le IG 18 KStN 1123 a (gp)

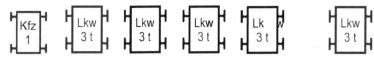

Panzerjäger-Zug with three 7.5cm PaK 40 KStN 1145 (gp)

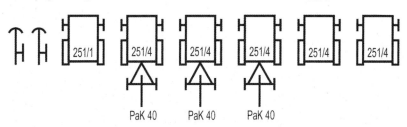

Type of soft-skinned vehicle depending on availability and theatre of war...
7.5cm PaK 40 could be substituted by 7.62cm PaK 36(r).

Schwere Kompanie
consisting of subunits, example PzAufklAbt 24, 24.PzDiv, 1943

schwerer Panzerspäh-Zug (7.5cm) KStN 1138

233	233	233	233	233	233	Lkw 3 t	Lkw 3 t
(7.5cm)	(7.5cm)	(7.5cm)	(7.5cm)	(7.5cm)	(7.5cm)		

schwerer Kanonen-Zug (7.5cm) KStN 1125 (gp)

251/3

251/9	251/9	251/9	251/9	251/9	251/9	251/1
(7.5cm)	(7.5cm)	(7.5cm)	(7.5cm)	(7.5cm)	(7.5cm)	(Mun)

Pionier-Zug 'a' (gp) KStN 1124 a (gp)

251/10
(3.7)

251/7	251/7	251/7	251/7	251/7

Lkw 3 t	Lkw 3 t	Lkw 3 t

On later production SdKfz 233, the side and rear armour of the fighting compartment was raised to improve the protection of the crew against infantry weapons and shrapnel.

Above: Winter of 1942 on the Russian battlefront: a late-series SdKfz 232 has become bogged down in a snow-covered, frozen water hazard. The crew in a similar vehicle attempt a recovery.

Right: Initially, the SdKfz 250/1 was armed with two 7.92mm MG 34, but towards the end of 1942 these were replaced by the more reliable, and effective, 7.92mm MG 42.

Above: The southern sector of the Eastern Front in the winter of 1942/43: The SdKfz 263 (Fu) often survived for a surprisingly long time on this battlefront, since they were not normally deployed on or in the vicinity of the frontline.

Left: This SdKfz 250/9 has been almost completely destroyed by light artillery fire. Due to the constant shortage of spare parts, a group of field engineers has searched through the wreckage to recover any usable items.

Modern Reconnaissance

In the spring of 1943, the merging of the KradSchtz battalions with AufklAbt (mot) was largely completed. This basically provided the reconnaissance elements with a much greater combat strength, since the KradSchtz were now being successively equipped with light SchtzKp or light AufklKp in accordance with KStN 111 (gp), issued with armoured personnel carriers.

Conversely, there was now a danger that the PzAufklKp in cooperation with the battalion would now use the KradSchtz/PzGren as an actual combat force. Thus, their original purpose as tactical/operational reconnaissance assets within the PzDiv was at least endangered.

On 1 March 1943 Guderian, whom Hitler had relieved of his post as commander of Panzergruppe 2 in December 1941 because of serious conflicts, was called back to active duty and assigned as the inspector of the armoured forces. Four weeks later, the *schnelle Truppen* was to be officially reorganized under the designation *Panzertruppe*.

The *Infanterie-Regimenter* (*motorisiert*) (InfRgt [mot] – infantry regiments [motorized]), which were part of the motorized infantry divisions, had already been renamed grenadier regiments in October 1942. This was followed in April 1943 by the transfer of the InfDiv (mot) to the *Panzertruppen* area of responsibility. At the same time, it was renamed PzGrenDiv.

The reconnaissance troops were also affected significantly by these changes. The former SchtzBtl were now renamed PzAufklAbt.

This table shows all PzAufklAbt and their subunits in their different organizational forms as of 1 May 1943. The renaming transfer of the InfDiv (mot) to PzGrenDiv has not yet been implemented. In addition to the active Panzer divisions, the table also shows the units of *Heeresgruppe Afrika* (Army Group Africa), SS units, and the elite InfDiv GD and

Opposite: July 1944: The crew of a late production SdKfz 231/1 from 12.SS-PzDiv *Hitlerjugend* take a rest amongst the rubble of shattered buildings in a bombed-out city (Caen) on the Normandy battlefront. The antenna on the left-hand side of the turret indicates that the vehicle carries a FuSprech 'f'.

AHA/In 6 Nr: 560/43 g. Kdos.   Geheime Kommando

Gliederung der Panzer-Aufklärungs-Able.

Pz. Div.	Pz. Aufkl. Abt.	Gliederung	Zugehörigkeit am 1.5.43	Veränderungen seit 1.5.43	Planungen und Bemerkungen	Pz. Div.	Pz. Aufkl. Abt.
1.	1		A.O.K. 15			15.	15
2.	2		A.O.K. 9			21.	21
3.	3		Pz. A.O.K. 4			90.le. Afr.	5
4.	4		A.O.K. 2			164.le. Afr.	16
5.	5		Pz. A.O.K. 3				9.
6.	6		Armee Gr. Hollidt			J.D. (mot)	
7.	7		Armee Gr. Hollidt			3.	16
8.	8		Pz. A.O.K. 3			10.	
9.	9		A.O.K. 9			16.	13
10.	10		Pz. A.O.K. 5			18.	
11.	11		Armee Gr. Hollidt			20.	
12.	12		Pz. A.O.K. 3			22. J.D.	
13.	13		A.O.K. 17			25.	
14.	14					29.	
16.	16					60.	
17.	17		Pz. A.O.K. 4				
18.	18		Pz. A.O.K. 2			⚡ A.H.	
19.	19		H. Gru. B			⚡-Pz. Gr. Reich	
20.	20		A.O.K. 9			⚡-Pz. Gr. T	
23.	23		Pz. A.O.K. 4			⚡-Pz. Gr. Wiking	
24.	24					J.D. G.D.	G
25.	25		A.O.K. Norwegen			H. Göring	
26.	26		A.O.K. 15				

50 Ausfertigungen
10. Ausfertigung. 158

en des Feldheeres Stand: 1.5.43.

Anlage 1 zu 2 St./43 p/2
Pz Offz b Chef Gen Std H

Gliederung	Zugehörigkeit am 1.5.43	Veränderungen seit 1.5.43	Planungen und Bemerkungen
	H. Gru. Afrika		
	"		
	"		
	"		
	Pz. A.O.K. 5		
	SS-Pz. Korps H. Gru. Süd		
	SS-Pz. Korps H. Gru. Süd		
	H. Gru. D		
	Pz. A.O.K. 4		

The allocation and organizational structures of all armoured reconnaissance battalions in May 1943.

InfDiv Hermann Göring (HG) formations. The table also reveals the number of PzSpKp 'c' equipped with SdKfz 250/9 (seven) as well as that of PzSpKp 'b' equipped with a single *Luchs*. The remaining KradSchtzKp were probably mostly equipped with the *Kübelwagen*. However, this cannot be verified.

From a report sent by PzAufklAbt 3 in April 1943:

SdKfz 250: A mechanical and tactical experience report.

The upcoming development shows that a considerably larger number of SdKfz 250 will be used within the armoured reconnaissance. For this reason, in the following remarks I will deal with the basic mechanical problems that have become apparent in the light armoured reconnaissance company (*) during a year of the toughest operations in the East. Our suggestions can help to make the vehicle even more efficient and resistant. It cannot be emphasized enough that the SdKfz 250 was, on the whole, a complete success, since the vehicle performed better than expected. This is proven by the 24 armoured personnel carriers of the original of the 37, which were delivered in April 1942, remain in service today. They have covered 10,000km to 15,000km so far, an unprecedented performance for an armoured tracked vehicle.

A standard PzSpKp 'c' was issued with 16 SdKfz 250/9. The rapid-firing 2cm KwK 38 L/55 gave the unit a weapon feared by enemy forces. The vehicle is in service with the PzAufklAbt of 5.SS-PzDiv *Wiking*.

Engine: The engine has proved to be very good. No major complaints have occurred, even though an average of over 10,000km have been covered. At the general overhaul in April 1943, the engines did not need to be replaced, and current experience suggests that they will stand the coming years' service.

Clutch: There are no particular complaints to report.

Transmission: The semi-automatic Variorex gearbox, which allows full utilization of the engine power due to its reduction gears, has proven itself to be excellent. The good off-road capability, manoeuvrability and speed are mainly due to the transmission.

Front Axle: Steering knuckle fractures occurred frequently from the beginning, especially on the left side. Steering knuckles [ball joints] and disc wheels are also too weak. As the vehicles aged, the bending and subsequent fractures increased to an unsustainable level. The front spring fatigues quickly. While no breaks occurred, this caused the front of the vehicle to drop very low, which also caused the drive sprocket to drop lower and lower. In many cases, it was at the level of the first running wheel. When driving off-road, the drive sprocket is thus exposed to dangerous impacts. This problem is only due to the disadvantageous position of the centre of gravity on the

Winter of 1943/44: Although weakly armoured, the SdKfz 250/9 was often deployed near the frontline to observe or provide support fire. This vehicle, camouflaged with white-wash paint is from the PzSpTrupp in 13.PzDiv.

Civilian vehicles were still being supplied to armoured divisions in 1944, since the number of VW *Typ* 166 *Schwimmwagen* required could never be delivered. The SdKfz 250/9 is in service with 5.SS-PzDiv *Wiking*.

SdKfz 250, which is not on the tracks, but for the most part on the front axle. Six SdKfz 10 type D7 have been running at the division since the beginning of the Russian campaign. The type represent the most mechanically reliable vehicle in the division. In contrast to the SdKfz 250, no damage to the front axle has occurred. Although the increased weight of the armoured superstructure certainly has an influence on the SdKfz 250, the problem is due to the fact that the running gear is shortened by one roller.

Suspension: The suspension showed major signs of wear after only 2,000km to 3,000km due to the poor road conditions. The fault lies in the NUL 40 bearings.

Fuel Tank: The fuel tank on the SdKfz 250 is made of sheet steel which is not, as it usually is, zinc plated. It is only protected against corrosion by a coating of chassis paint. This coating is dissolved by the fuel after some time and the paint particles clog diaphragms in fuel pumps. To prevent this, the tanks must not be emptied below 40 litres in service. This NOT acceptable for a combat vehicle.

Armour: Practice has shown that the SdKfz 250 light armoured personnel carrier in action is no longer a pure transport vehicle that takes the gunners into action. Rather, the vehicle is used as a dedicated combat vehicle. In the past year, only one assault was driven in a purely infantry manner; in all other cases, mounted combat was used for escorting a massed tanks assault.

After the breakthrough, the troops dismounted to clear enemy foxholes under the fire cover from their vehicles. A similar approach was taken during local engagements. As a result, the half-tracks, like the tanks, were exposed to enemy fire.

Most unpleasant, however, has proved to be fire from anti-tank rifles which led to major failures. Reinforcing the armour does not seem possible for weight reasons. Incidentally, the failures were primarily due to fire from the right flank. Bullets coming from the left very often got stuck ineffectively or detonated in the laundry bags, stowed inside, after penetrating the armour. The weapon mounts are attached to the right inner side which stiffens the plating. Experiments with spaced armour filled with pressed wool or similar fibrous materials have not yet been confirmed by practical tests. This consideration should be subjected to a technical review.

Likewise, it seems possible to further increase the angle of individual armour plates. A flatter angle of impact would presumably reduce the probability of penetration.

The SdKfz 250 is designed to carry six riflemen. Since it has been shown that most of the fighting was done from and with the vehicle, this number is considered too high. The men get in the way of one another, and four crew members would appear to be sufficient. This would also reduce personnel losses in the event of hits.

Spring 1945, the final battle for Berlin: An SdKfz 250/1 lies abandoned next to one of the many 8.8cm FlaK positioned around the city to halt the waves of Red Army tanks.

Armament: In the future, the MG 42 should be used as on-board machine gun. The effect, both morally and practically, would be incomparably higher. It would also simplify barrel changes in the cramped interior. It has proved expedient to equip all vehicles (not only the PaK and mortar carriers) with swivel arms to use the MG against attacks by hostile aircraft. The arms must be mounted not only at the rear, but also at the sides, so that the second machine gun carried can be used from the vehicle during combat. This is especially important when breaking into enemy positions to achieve maximum weapon effectiveness. The 3.7cm PaK does not provide anti-tank defence in the true sense, but can still be used as a heavy weapon in infantry combat. Since its rate of fire is too low for the changing operational methods of a company, we call for a switch to heavy long-range machine guns. Instead of the 3.7cm PaK, the 2cm KwK 30 L/55 in a similar mount could be used. As a heavy weapon, the 7.5cm KwK 37 L/24 already mounted in the SdKfz 251 should soon be included in our inventory. (**)

This would require a change in the relevant KStN organizational structure. The heavy platoon, still structured along the lines of the earlier non-armoured rifle company, has proved impractical in its present form. The heavy MG has practically never been used in the SdKfz 250 in the form intended. In practice, there is no significant difference in firing accuracy between an MG mounted in the armoured gun shield with a centre support and the heavy MG mounting. For this reason, the heavy carriage is redundant. (***)

A maintenance crew work to replace an idler wheel. The track and running on the SdKfz 250 and SdKfz 251 half-track vehicles required almost daily intensive maintenance.

If the vehicle is equipped with 7.5cm KwK 37 L/24, the s GrW can also be abandoned. This would make the heavy platoon unnecessary. (****)

Periscope: The periscope is part of the basic equipment on the vehicle, but it is never used and must be considered unnecessary.

Ammunition Stowage: The position of the ammunition box is ridiculous on two counts. The side-mounted door cannot be opened in combat without seriously hindering the fighting crew. It is suggested that the door be mounted on the front of the ammunition box. The shape of the box should be adapted to that of the superstructure, so that the dead space behind it would be used appropriately.

Flare Stowage: It has been shown in practice that the box intended for the storage of illumination ammunition is not needed.

Cartridge Cases: A bag should be produced and fitted on both machine guns to catch spent cartridge cases. These often fall around the gearbox and can jam the gearshift levers. Also, the driver can be seriously affected by any hot ammunition cases falling on his neck.

This SdKfz 250/5 Ausf A still carries the conspicuous frame-type antenna for the Fu 12 radio. Note the front MG 34 is fitted with a non-standard armoured gun shield.

Radio-equipped SdKfz 250: It has already been shown in the first missions that the radio-equipped half-track [leader's vehicle] fitted with the rigid frame antenna is easily recognized by the enemy as a command vehicle and is immediately taken under fire. The radio car [SdKfz 250/3] and often receives the highest number of hits in the company. It has therefore proved expedient to equip the vehicles with a folding frame antenna (similar to the small armoured radio car [SdKfz 223]). This modification should be put into series production immediately. (*****)

Towards the end of the war, the PzSpKp 'e' was issued with a platoon of SdKfz 251/21 *Drilling* (triple). These vehicles had tremendous firepower being armed with three (either 15mm MG 151/15 or 2cm MG151/20) aircraft-type autocannons. Although originally produced to defend against ground-attack aircraft, the SdKfz 251/21 proved to be very effective for ground combat.

(*) The KStN was valid for both le SchtzKp (gp) and le AufklKp (gp).

(**) This requirement was soon to be implemented.

(***) MG 34 and MG 42 could be fired from a recoil suppressor-type mounting as a 'heavy' machine gun, or used on a tripod mount.

(****) As far as is known, this requirement was not implemented. However, it was in the hands of the division commander and also the company commander to restructure the individual platoons on a case-by-case basis.

(*****) During 1942, the conspicuous frame antenna was replaced by a *Sternantenne* 'd'. Apparently, older vehicles SdKfz 250/3 were not automatically re-equipped at front-line units. However, the troops knew how to improvize.

On 1 May 1944, the commander of PzAufklAbt 23 prepared a comprehensive field report describing the deployment of the 2.Kp, which was reorganized in November 1943 to the new structure PzAufklKp 'c' (KStN 1162 c).

His report shows that reconnaissance battalions in the field were often used for other tasks. He also specifically addresses delaying operations in the context of making a controlled attack.

Spring 1944: An SdKfz 250/5 of an unknown unit during the fighting in Stanyslaviv [Ivano-Frankivsk], shortly before the Red Army launched *Operatsiya* (Operation) *Bagration* on 22 June 1944. The vehicle is leading a reconnaissance squad.

A tank division retreated fighting from position to position as part of an infantry corps. To do this, the unit had to defend both the strip of movement and, in defence, also from dug-in positions. The division had weak PzGren elements and one PzPiBtl, but due to a lack of transport capacity, these battalions could only be moved in multiple rides. In addition to these forces, the PzAufklAbt fought with a PzSpKp 'c', a KradSchtzKp, and a truck-mounted reconnaissance company, but no heavy company. The PzAbt and the bulk of the PzGrenBtl in our PzDiv were deployed elsewhere as corps reserves. Due to the lack of mobility, the dismounted movements required special organization. Here the PzAufklAbt did a remarkable job. First, it was placed close (about 3km) behind the *Hauptkampflinie* (HKL – main battle line) and formed a reception for the PzGren marching back on foot, whose movements it effectively secured and concealed. In the further course of the retreat, the PzAufklAbt then went back to the new HKL in short stages, always fighting, to be used in an advanced position or as a combat outpost. After completing its mission in front of the HKL, the battalion was sent to the rear to

Above: The introduction of the 8-Rad (Tp) marked a turning point. Even though supplying reconnaissance units with half – and fully tracked vehicles had priority due to their better cross-country mobility, these heavy armoured reconnaissance vehicles had a far better range.

Right: After proving to be effective when mounted in the SdKfz 250/9 Ausf B, it was decided that the 2cm KwK 38 L/55 would be installed in the SdKfz 234/1 using a suspended mount.

rest and resupply. If the retreat movements continued, the battalions fought again in the same manner. For this purpose, the PzAufklAbt was assigned a battery 2cm FlaK 38 L/55 on SdKfz 10/4, a company 7.5cm PaK 40 L/48 [*Marder*] and a light field howitzer battery. This formation, especially the assignment of the light howitzers, proved to be expedient.

Our PzSpKp 'c' was assigned a special task during these retreat movements. Often directly attached to the division, it provided armoured reconnaissance squads that reconnoitered in neighbouring division sectors. In this way, the PzDiv could be continuously informed of the enemy's attacking spearheads and of any incursions that had been made. The result: during the retreat no surprising, dangerous situations arose at any time. PzSpKp 'c', reinforced by PzJg on Sfl, was used with great success several times for surprise thrusts against the flanks of the enemy's attacking spearheads or advance divisions. Apart from the fact that this offensive advance inflicted considerable losses on the enemy, its attack was delayed. The PzGren gained valuable time to establish themselves in their own positions and dig in.

This use of the PzAufklAbt kept the enemy away from the HKL almost twice as long as the neighboring infantry divisions, If the enemy hit the HKL, it was fully defended by PzGren from their carefully prepared dug-in positions.

This report shows that in emergencies the reconnaissance elements were capable of tasks that contradicted their operational purpose. The attachment of other subunits and weapons turned the PzAufklAbt into a combat group.

Organizational Issues

With the implementation of the Panzer Division 44 organizational structure, the PzAufklAbt was also to receive its final equipment and organization. The combat companies were now equipped throughout with half-track vehicles, SdKfz 250 and SdKfz 251 in their various forms and variants.

The staff company (KStN 1109), conversly, also had wheeled armoured reconnaissance vehicles. While the mass of the PzAufklAbt (four combat companies) were equipped with more effective armoured half-track vehicles, with better cross-country mobility, the wheeled armoured reconnaissance vehicles of the *Stabs-Kompanie* (StbsKp – staff company) had a higher speed and a much longer range of up to 1,000km (depending on the type).

In November 1944, the the StbsKp was initially equipped differently. A StbsKp Ausf A had three light platoons issued with SdKfz 222 and Sdkfz 223, while a StbsKp Ausf B had two heavy platoons, each with four SdKfz 234/1 or SdKfz 234/3. These heavy armoured reconnaissance vehicles could

The PzSpWg II Ausf L *Luchs* was a reconnaissance vehicle with outstanding mobility and a road speed of 60kph. The vehicle weighed 11,800kg and was powered by a 6,754cc Maybach HL66 P six-cylinder water-cooled petrol engine driving a *Zahnradfabrik Friedrichshafen* (ZF) SSG 48 six-speed gearbox.

be replaced by SdKfz 232, if still available. In practice there were probably also mixed configurations. It is quite possible that the staff companies were supplied with SdKfz 234/1 and Sdkfz 234/2 in addition to older stocks of SdKfz 232 and Sdkfz 233.

The available organization tables for PzAufklAbt show this element in the

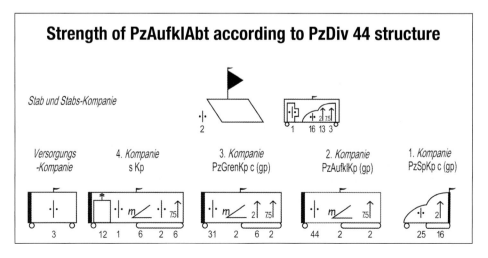

Strength of PzAufklAbt according to PzDiv 44 structure

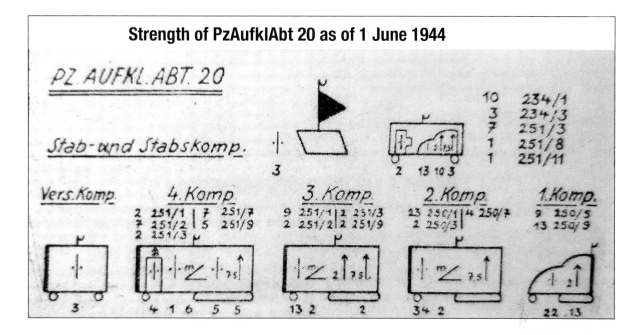

Strength of PzAufklAbt 20 as of 1 June 1944

staff companies in platoon strength, which deviated from the KStN, which showed two or three platoons. It must be repeated that the material equipment issued was, as always, dependent on the general situation and the availability of modern equipment.

- Stab- and StbsKp to KStN 1109.
- PzSpKp 'c' to KStN 1113 (c).
- le PzAufklKp (gp) to KStN 1113 (gp).
- PzAufklKp 'c' (gp) to KStN 1114 (c) (gp).
- Heavy Company (with subunits).
- *Versorgungs-Kompanie* (supply company).

In February 1945, the *Generalinspekteur der Panzertruppe* (GenInsp d PzTrp – inspector general of armoured forces) urged more accuracy in content of the regularly submitted status reports. A sample report sent by PzAufklAbt 20 was printed as a guide (date unknown). This clearly shows the equipment available, but the indicated numbers can deviate from the target strengths of the individual subunits. All wartime strength statements indicated in the notations that designated equipment could be replaced by older material. Thus, instead of NSU *Kettenkrads* (SdKfz 2), standard motorcycles could be assigned, and instead of the modern SdKfz 234/1 and SdKfz 234/3, existing SdKfz 231, SdKfz 232 and SdKfz 233 could also be assigned.In October 1944, the inspector general specified the operational principles of the armoured reconnaissance battalions:

Above: The 5cm KwK 39/1 L/60 mounted in the SdKfz 234/2 *Puma* gave the reconnaissance vehicle very effective firepower. After 100 vehicles had been produced, the more versatile 2cm KwK 38 L/55 was installed and fitted on a *Hängelafette*.

Right: The successes of the SdKfz 250/8, SdKfz 251/9 and also the SdKfz 233, led to the installation of the 7.5cm KwK L/24 in the 8-Rad (Tp). A total of 90 SdKfz 234/3 had been built by the end of 1944.

Above: The SdKfz 234/2 *Puma* 'not only had excellent performance on hard-packed road surfaces, but also had cross-country mobility which fully-met the demands of the reconnaissance units.

Left: The 7.5cm K 1 allowed the engagement of soft and semi-hard targets even with HE ammunition at a range of up to 6,500m. The 7.5cm *Granate-Hohlladung* (GrHl – hollow-charge shell) 38 type C was effective against enemy armour.

Evaluation of a field report from 4.PzDiv in the East: How operational and tactical reconnaissance is executed

Air reconnaissance
Ground reconnaissance

Since under present conditions the Panzer division or higher command authorities have only a few reconnaissance aircraft at their disposal, the Panzer division is today more than ever dependent on the reconnaissance by its PzAufklAbt. The use of this element for its actual task, the 'reconnaissance', is of increased importance especially in unsettled and critical situations. However, if the reconnaissance detachment is used incorrectly (as a 'fire brigade' of the division or corps), it is not available for its actual task. The combat troops are then forced to operate on their own with their own few suitable assets, which unduly weakens their combat power.

In the defence against large-scale enemy attacks, however, the PzAufklAbt is an indispensable means to our higher command levels. Here it is deployed as a mobile fighting unit for the breakthrough. However, it does not have to fight dismounted in order to block an incursion.

The PzAufklAbt must always keep contact with the enemy and constantly monitor his movements. Detachments deployed in accordance with these principles have always been able to prevail successfully in combat and provide their Panzer division with the necessary command and control information. PzAufklAbt 4 in 4.PzDiv also fought successfully for four weeks on these principles. It kept 80 percent of its equipment operational during this time, despite non-stop action with little time or opportunity for repair.

Field report on the combat deployment of the 2.PzSpKp 'c'/PzAufklAbt 23 from 9 March to 25 April 1944

Build-up Phase: On 18 November 1943, 2./PzAufklAbt 23 was transferred to the military training area Senne for reorganization and rearmament as PzPsKp 'c'. The

Strength of PzAufklAbt 4 as of 1 January 1944

company was until then a light company and brought almost all the required personnel with it, except for drivers, gunners (*) and radio operators. The transport to Russia took place on 18 February 1944, but delivery of the vehicles, weapons and the replacement of personnel took place over a relatively long period due to many delays. So much so that combat training could not be carried out, which meant that field readiness was achieved only with great difficulty.

1.) Personnel situation: The replacements brought in were insufficiently trained. As a result, in-depth retraining became necessary, especially with regard to operations in the East. The drivers and radio operators arrived on January 21, which allowed us only 12 days to retrain them on the operation of the vehicles and equipment.
2.) Motor vehicles: All, without exception, were delivered in perfect operational condition.
3.) Experiences in the previous deployment: The company rejoined 23.PzDiv on 5 March 1944, and was deployed southwest of Krivoy Rog. Initially it had been deployed to Kasanke as a division reserve. The use of armoured reconnaissance units was impossible due the thick and deep mud that prevailed as the snow and ice melted. During the retreat from the Bug river towards Vossnessensk, which began on March 9, the company was deployed as part of the armoured combat group. (**) This was practically formed from 2.Kp alone, since there were practically no operational tanks,

In January 1945, Adolf Hitler issued an explicit order for the 7.5cm PaK 40 to be installed in the SdKfz 251 and also 8-Rad reconnaissance vehicles. The result was the SdKfz 251/22 and the SdKfz 234/4; both had the firepower to defeat all enemy medium tanks.

Budapest 1945: a column of vehicles from a PzSpKp 'e' (13.PzDiv) abandoned in a street after German forces became trapped in the Hungarian capital. Among the vehicles are several SdKfz 251/21 *Drillings-Wagen,* each mounting three 2cm anti-aircraft cannons, which were feared by enemy forces due their high firepower.

Early in the war, the *Panzergrenadier* (PzGren – armoured infantry) demanded an armoured vehicle for evacuating casualties from the battlefield. The result was a special variant of the medium armoured half-track being produced: the SdKfz 251/8 *mittlere Kranken-Panzerwagen* medium armoured ambulance.

assault guns, or armoured half-tracks and other vehicles left in the division. The operation was limited, firstly, to reconnaissance deep into the right flank of enemy forces advancing on Nikolaev. Secondly, attacks by our reinforced tank reconnaissance units on Panje [*Panjeskaya*] horse-drawn columns to disrupt his supply routes. We were assigned three SdKfz 124 *Wespe* [wasp], two SdKfz 165 *Hummel* [bumblebee] and two 7.5cm PaK L/48, which allowed the company to achieve a great success in these tasks despite the most difficult terrain conditions. We also obtained good reconnaissance results.

Due to the failure of almost all means of communication at the battalion, and also the PzDiv, regulated scouting patrols by the battalion could not take place. In addition, the division was deployed to completely different sections of the front. The *Kampfgruppe* [battle group] was often attached to various other units, and because of the situation, was often forced to operate without definitive orders. The commander's vehicle, as well as the radio cars of the reconnaissance squads, were not needed to relay radio communications. It has been shown that the training of radio operators must be given the utmost importance. The men must have a high level of physical and mental toughness so that they can withstand the stresses of a day-long operation. After a transfer, by rail, to the area north of the river Pruth and near Jassi, completely different requirements arose during the fighting. From 5 April 1944, we were almost exclusively deployed for combat missions.

The SdKfz 251/8 could accommodate either four stretcher-bound casualties or up to ten seated. This vehicle is a standard SdKfz 251/1 which has been converted at a field workshop unit attached to PzAufklAbt 4. It was not standard to arm a medical vehicle (here with an MG 34) but it was probably felt to be necessary on the Eastern Front.

Due to the mountainous terrain, operations were carried out in platoon strength and were supported by infantry, as well as self-propelled, and towed anti-tank guns and assault guns. The enemy advancing from Balti, was holding positions just a few kilometers north of the bridges over the Pruth at Ungheni after cutting the main road from Kishinev to Yassi. The soft ground was heavily rutted and many areas still remained under a covering of thick snow; great caution had to be taken even on paved roads and gravel-surfaced tracks. The *Kampfgruppe*, deployed in the same configuration as above, was tasked with clearing those enemy forces holding the main road to allow safe passage for the fast divisions (23.PzDiv, 24.PzDiv and InfDiv [GD]) coming from the north.

The company, despite the difficult terrain and low combat strength (two assault guns, a weak infantry company of 35 men, five SdKfz 250/9 and a radio car), managed to knock-out 13 enemy tanks of the type General Sherman [US-built M4A-2] without any losses, and push the enemy back into the mountains. The reasons for this were:

- The opponent was hit hard by our determined attack,
- Our forces were prepared to leave paved roads,
- Soft points observed in enemy positions were attacked, at lightning speed and long fire range, by our 2cm weapons.

It has been shown that the 2cm FlaK 38 L/55 gun is extremely feared by the Russian infantry. Even enemy anti-tank guns, also tanks, keep moving out of range, but any

Above: Existing photographs of the 8-Rad (Tp) show that they were not fitted with heavily treaded cross-country tyres, incomprehensible for an all-terrain military vehicle.

Right: The large aperture in the gun mantlet was for the coaxially mounted MG 42, the smaller one in the turret was for a TZF 4b sighting telescope. The SdKfz 234/2 was built in 1943 and has a *Nebelkurzen-Abwurfvorrichtung* (NKAV – smoke grenade dispenser) on the turret.

that are recognized by our gunners are quickly and effectively knocked out. The prerequisite for this is that the vehicle commander and his crew have been well trained for combat operations, and are alert to the situation on the battlefront where they must be prepared, due to changing conditions, to take independent action.

In the battles on the road from Kishinev to Yassi, north of the Pruth, the half-track armoured reconnaissance vehicles proved to be an outstanding asset; their transition from reconnaissance to combat tasks was accomplished smoothly. The decisive factor for this was the versatility and excellent training of new personnel supported by a number of highly experienced veteran armoured reconnaissance troopers.

A third section deployed for this mission was engaged in the defensive battles north of Jassi. Here our armoured scout cars were used as 'eyes on the enemy' at important points behind the frontline and for battlefield observation behind the flanks of the two divisions. The scout cars reported continuously on the enemy situation and on the dispersion of Romanian regiments, which were very unpredictable during this period. In many cases the reconnaissance units formed interception points for the retreating Romanians, and more than once, acting independently and recognizing the danger of the situation, they pushed Romanian units forward again into new positions. The deployment of the entire company in the heavily rutted and mountainous terrain was never possible because of too little freedom of movement. In the foothills of the Carpathians, there are hardly any operational possibilities for a larger tank unit, which

This top view of a SdKfz 243/2 shows a 1.4m rod antenna and the turret ventilator which was installed under the round grating next to the antenna base. A *Turm-Beobachtungsfernrohr* (TBF – turret observation periscope) 14 is positioned in front of the open commander's hatch.

A *Kradmelder* on a Zündapp motorcycle studying a map. Despite the fact that from 1942 the reconnaissance units had better vehicles, such as the *Kübelwagen* and *Schwimmwagen* at their disposal, the *Beiwagen-Kräder* continued to be used until the end of the war.

is always tied to roads and tracks. The enemy is so adept at shifting his anti-tank units during attack – or counterattack – that he succeeds in using his accurate shooting and long-range anti-tank weapons to devastating effect. Under these circumstances, any attack involving the use of a PzSpKp 'c' requires a thorough prior reconnaissance of the terrain and surrounding environs.

The PzSpKp 'c' squads are far better suited for reconnaissance in the current area of operations than squads issued with wheeled vehicle, as they are much more able to overcome the difficult terrain.

The following can be said about the mechanical performance of the PzSpWg 'c' (SdKfz 250/9): The half-track vehicle is not up to the exceptionally deep mud experienced of spring and autumn. If the mud is soft and fluid, progress is easy. But as the soil dries, a heavy thick mush is created, and this clogs the drive and running wheels which become locked causing tracks to fail. Also, the consumption of rubber track pads when running on the road increases at an alarming rate.

The ground clearance is too low due to the weight of the *Panzeraufbau*. It would be worth considering whether this can be remedied by installing larger wheels. As a

The observation officer of a SdKfz 250/5 searches the terrain through a *Scherenfernrohr* (SF – scissors telescope) 14. The device had a 10x magnification and allowed the measurement of lateral and elevation angles.

result of the extra load, the rubber banding on the running wheels became loose after about 50km. This problem was solved by drilling four holes in each.

The pistons of the steering brakes seize up because they have been lubricated incorrectly. The steering ball joints have proven to be too weak when subjected to heavy loads on uneven terrain and often bend before breaking off at the stub axle. The steering push rod is also particularly vulnerable because it is mounted too low. When driving over small tree stumps or other obstacles, the steering can only be turned in one direction, due to the bracket for the idler arm is poorly attached, being held in place by only three spot welds. Consequently, it cannot withstand the heavy load exerted by the track tensioner and regularly tears off. By adding more spot welds, to prevent the item failing.

The brake pads wore out too quickly. Apparently, this is caused by the penetration of dirt and mud; an effective seal is required. The brake lining (poor quality material) becomes permeated very quickly with oil which causes a loss of braking.

The radio equipment is insufficient. Any communication between the vehicle commander and his driver is not possible in combat due to engine and other

A VW *Typ* 166 *Schwimmwagen:* the three-bladed propeller propulsion assembly is visible on the rear of the vehicle. When entering the water, this was lowered and engaged.

mechanical noises. The company has constructed an on-board intercom system during their training period at the Staumühlen Camp. Furthermore, the installation of a second receiver and also a high-frequency radio are required for the commander's vehicle. This would allow communication between the tanks and the leader of the PzSpKp during assault operations. This equipment should be fitted to all PzSpWg 'c' during production.

Summary: The PzSpWg 'c' has proved its worth in the first two months of the company's deployment in Russia, both in reconnaissance and in combat operations. The minor mechanical deficiencies encountered take a back seat to the major advantages; both the veteran scout crews on wheels (wheeled reconnaissance cars) and those experienced half-track crews now have full confidence in their new weapon, despite initial reservations.

(*) This example shows how long the old designation *Schützen* remained in use.

(**) The term *Kampfgruppe* is somewhat misleading since 23.PzDiv had practically no tanks in April 1944, because the II./PzRgt 23, a PzKpfw V *Panther*-equipped battalion, was attached to a different army corps.

This report was printed in the *Nachrichtenblatt für die Panzertruppe* in July 1944. The *Generalinspekteur der Panzertruppe* wrote in the commentary:

> From the field report of the battalion, it is clear that the half-track-equipped reconnaissance company 'c' remains mobile even in difficult terrain and despite muddy conditions and has achieved good results. The described cooperation with *Wespe* and *Hummel* does not correspond to the operational methods of self-propelled artillery. The example described is an exception and must not become the rule.
>
> The success of the five PzSpWg, supported only by a weak infantry company of 35 men and also two assault guns, deserves a special mention. This example is proof that where the Russian is attacked decisively, he can be beaten even with small forces. The reconnaissance company 'c', thanks to its all-terrain capability, is better suited to the solution of combat and reconnaissance tasks than the wheeled scout company. For the performance of combat tasks, it is advantageous to reinforce the armoured reconnaissance squad with assault guns for protection against enemy tanks.

The reference to reinforcing armoured reconnaissance squads with assault guns or tanks presupposes, of course, the availability of these armoured vehicles. In the case described, parts of an army StuGAbt that happened to be in the area were probably subordinated. It may be assumed that in the last year of the war every possibility was resorted to, including self-propelled artillery. The strength report of 1 April 1944 shows the very mixed equipment of PzAufklAbt 23; wheeled armoured reconnaissance vehicles, half-track armoured reconnaissance vehicles and light and medium armoured personnel carriers.

After the tank battle at Debrecen (Hungary) in September 1944, PzAufklAbt 23 (23.PzDiv) delivered a field report:

PzAufklAbt (gp) reconnaissance and attack:

22 September 1944: After the conclusion of the tank battle at Debrecen, the enemy continued to advance northward and reached the area within the Theiss (Tisza) arc near Szap (Tschop) with reconnaissance forces on 22 October 1944. These forces blocked or threatened the retreat routes of an army group.

On 22 October 1944, PzAufklAbt 23, attached to *Armee-Abteilung* Fretter-Pico, was being held in reserve at Munkacs (Mukatschewe).

At 13:40hrs the division received the following order from the army group: Clearance of the Theiss arc and attack the enemy reconnaissance forces in the area of Dombrad, Vasaros (Vásárosnamény), Namény and Szap. Then continue further reconnaissance up to the line of Tokaj, Nyíregyháza and Mate-Szalka (Mátászalka).

At 14:05hrs, three 8-Rad reconnaissance squads started toward this line: the PzAufklAbt without 3.Kp [SdkFz 251] marched on the road from Szap to Kis-Varda (Kisvárda) and Nyíregyháza. A scouting party deployed here reconnoitered immediately in front of the detachment. Then 3.Kp was ordered to advance along the road from Bergeszasz (Berehowe) to Vasaros where they were to establish a bridgehead across the Theiss river.

The bulk of the division reached Szap in the evening and established the required bridge over the river. At the same time, the 3.Kp formed, as ordered, a bridgehead at Vasaros.

The advance scouting party reported that the southern edge of Kis-Varda was occupied by the enemy (anti-tank guns and mortars). The battalion immediately marched towards the village, and 3.Kp was also ordered to advance. When the advance elements reached Kis-Varda, it met no more enemy resistance, as it had already been broken by the 2.Kp. Immediately a PzSpTrupp 'c' was deployed for further reconnaissance; the enemy had set up defensive positions south of the village, near to Ajak.

Strength of PzAufklAbt 23 as of April 1944

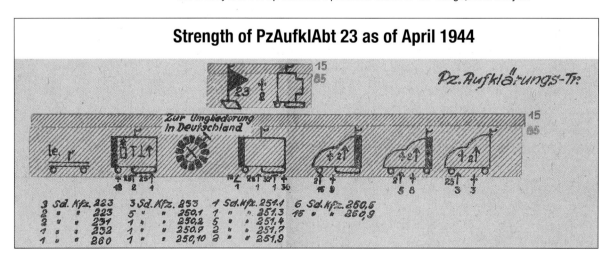

The commander decided that 4.hsKp would launch a head-on attack on the village, while the 3.Kp [SdKfz 251] pushed past Ajak and attacked the enemy from the rear. The 2.Kp [SdKfz 250] would then move in the direction of Dombrád.

The attack from the rear allowed enemy forces to escape to the south, but they were forced to abandon their heavy weapons including most of their tanks, anti-tank guns and rifles, light and heavy mortars and infantry weapons.

The mission to clear the Theiss Arc of enemy reconnaissance units had been accomplished. The enemy is now only holding Dombrád to the west of Kis-Varda. The 2.Kp (SdKfz 250) was on the march with orders to take Dombrád. The attack had to be halted, however, since the village was surrounded by a moat and was considered to be fully *panzersicher* [safe against a tank attack]. In addition, the company was subjected to shelling from several heavy anti-tank guns. Our casualty count was nil. Within 24 hours, the division marched 40km and cleared enemy reconnaissance units from a 30km deep corridor. In addition, successful wheeled reconnaissance (8-Rad [Tp]) was conducted over an area of 50km by some 60km. The division's command post, remained in Kis-Varda for the day. To secure the area, several PzSpTrupp 'c' were pushed to the south.

In the meantime, reconnaissance in the direction of Nyíregyháza revealed that the village of Nyirtass, and the fork in the road 2km to the west, was occupied by the

The SdKfz 2 *Kettenkrad* *Ketten* [tracks], *krad* [motorcycle]) had an excellent off-road performance. Originally intended for use in the snow, ice and deep mud on the *Ost* Front, it was actually used on all battlefronts.

enemy and we also observed seven enemy anti-tank guns in dug-in positions. Accurate reconnaissance information of the battlefront continued to be received until late on 23 September, as the division continued to make preparations for the attack to the south. In the early hours of 24 September 1944, the division's status changed. The *Heeresgruppe* now placed the battalion under the command of a *Kampfgruppe*, which included a AufklAbt of a light infantry division. The *Kampfgruppen* leader gave as the day's objective the seizure of Nyirtass, and the expected start to the attack was to begin at 14:00hrs. Before the attack, the commander of the PzAufklAbt reconnoitered the terrain on both sides of the main road and suggested that the attack be conducted from the east into the rear and flank of the enemy positions. After initial agreement, however, the *Kampfgruppen* leader decided to attack along the road. As justification he cited information from the army group that the enemy was escaping to the south. He ordered the battalion to attack immediately without proper deployment and preparation. The warnings issued by the commander of the PzAufklAbt that a frontal attack would be futile since a number of anti-tank guns had been positioned to protect the road.

Thus PzSpTrupp 'c' led the battalion on the advance with 3.Kp to the left of the road, and followed by elements of the staff company, then 2.Kp, 4.Kp, and 1.Kp. As enemy anti-tank guns opened fire, the first vehicles escaped being knocked-out only by highly skilled driving and, above all, pure luck. Immediately, the commander ordered 2.Kp to leave the road, swerve to the right and attempt to attack the guns. As a result of the PK barrage, the company had to move further out of range and did not rejoin the road until they were over a kilometre south of Nyirtass.

The commander now ordered the 2.Kp to regroup on the road in a hedgehog formation. The infantry of 3.Kp was ordered to dismount and launch a head-on attack against the anti-tank guns.

The enemy had been weakened by the threat of an attack from the rear and was easily routed, under the cover of darkness, by 3.Kp. The division captured several anti-tank guns and a number of light weapons without suffering any casualties. Nyirtass was then taken after difficult house-to-house fighting. Our losses were not significant.

During the night of 24-25 September 1944, reconnaissance was carried out in the direction of Nyíregyháza. Result: Berkesz and the heights eastward of it were occupied by the enemy, and four anti-tank guns were detected.

25 September 1944: In the morning hours PzAufklAbt 23 received orders to attack, without regard to threats from the flank and rear, and advance along the road toward Nyíregyháza. Again, a proposal by the commander to bypass the anti-tank blockade was rejected, and the leader of the battle group ordered the frontal attack. Artillery or assault gun support was not available. After the heavy weapons were brought into position, the battalion attacked Berkesz with 3.Kp on the right and 2.Kp on the left of

the road, which in turn was heavily mined and the terrain was riddled with abandoned trenches. The 2.Kp, mounted on armoured half-tracks, broke through the field positions in front of the village and cleared them in close combat.

The 3.Kp was pinned down just outside the village in front of a wide water obstacle, which was crossed by a single, but mined, bridge. The enemy anti-tank guns detected behind it were successfully held down by the SdKfz 251/9 of the *Kanonen-Zug*. Nevertheless, one of our own half-tracks was knocked-out. The leader of the 3.Kp succeeded in removing the mines on the bridge, making it possible for our troops to enter the village. This was captured after a short but vicious firefight first by mounted, later by dismounted troops. During this frontal attack, three of our carriers were knocked out by anti-tank guns, and also the commander of the lead platoon was seriously wounded.

The *Schwimmwagen* was powered by a 1,131cc air-cooled four-cylinder petrol engine which was not only reliable but also simple to maintain.

In 1944, the prototype of a tracked reconnaissance tank was built which utilized the hull, superstructure and other components from the *leichter Panzerjäger* (le PzJg – light tank destroyer) *Hetzer* (baiter). It is thought that two trials vehicles had been completed by May 1945 and that a variant armed with a 2cm KwK 38 L/55, in suspended mount, was also planned. But military officials decided priority was to be given to the PzJg 38(d).

After repelling a Russian counterattack, the village remained in the possession of the battalion, and the infantry battalion was now also called in to secure it. But, as a result of the frontal attack, the enemy managed to withdraw without any losing any weapons or equipment. According to prisoners, a Cossack regiment had been positioned in the village.

26 September 1944: The army group ordered an advance on Nyíregyháza and liaison with a Panzer division, which was also to approach the target from the southwest. Again, a frontal attack was ordered, which could only be prevented by the sharpest intervention of the commander of the PzAufklAbt.

The battalion now bypassed the mined road and travelled more to the west. On the evening of 26 September contact was be made with the PzDiv.

The *Generalinspekteur der Panzertruppe* emphasized in a statement that the PzAufklAbt was given tasks that corresponded to its status and equipment. Separated from the 23.PzDiv (the reasons are not known), the detachment was assigned other tasks by the command authorities. The use of the SdKfz 234 (8-Rad) PzSpWg was positively acclaimed. These were easily able to

provide reconnaissance results quickly over long distances on good roads. The SdKfz 250/9 of PzAufklKp 'c' supplemented this reconnaissance thanks to their superior cross-country mobility and effective armament.

In order to perform such demanding tasks, PzAufklAbt must necessarily be reinforced with anti-tank and artillery elements.

(Note, the abbreviation GPW in the diagram means *Grenadier-Panzerwagen*, and is synonymous with the SdKfz 250 and SdKfz 251. The designation *Panzergrenadier-Wagen* (PGW) was also used until the end of the war.)

Two VW *Typ* 82 *Kübelwagen* from the KradSchtzAbt in 1.SS-PzDiv LAH. The light vehicles could carry four fully equipped soldiers, and despite the lack of all-wheel drive their off-road capability was legendary.

Western Front

The situation in the west after the Allied landings, on 6 June 1944, was completely different. In addition to the invaders being militarily superior, the German defenders faced, due to the lack of fighter protection, frequent deadly strikes by Allied ground-attack aircraft. Much of this is detailed in the war diary of PzAufklAbt 11 (11.PzDiv) preserved in the archives.

The 11.PzDiv had been transferred from the Eastern Front to the west for rest re-equipment and reorganization at the end of May 1944. This process had not yet been completed in June and, according to the judgment of its commander, the motorized elements were only 20 to 30 percent ready and he described the unit as having limited operational capability. Of the target inventory of 811 PzKpfw IV, 61 were operational, but the PzKpfw V *Panther*-equipped battalion issued with 79 tanks was completely missing. Only 84 cross-country cars, were available to the division whereas the target was 578. The disparity in cross-country trucks was even greater, 53 against a target of 925.

In early June, the division was at Catillon, near Bordeaux. After the Allied landings, the PzAufkl units were engaged in fierce fighting with French partisan forces, who had noticeably increased their activities before the 6 June.

Vehicles of a PzAufklAbt during the retreat from French territory in autumn 1944. The crew of this SdKfz 250/1 has fitted a 1939-style spare running wheel to the front of the vehicle.

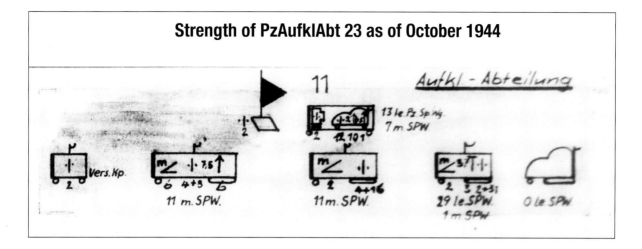

Strength of PzAufklAbt 23 as of October 1944

On 1 June, PzAufklAbt 11 had:

Stabskompanie (gp) with *Nachrichten-Zug* and two weak PzSpZg to KStN 1109 (gp).
PzSpKp 'c' to KStN 1162 (c) without any SchtzPz.
le PzSpKp (gp) to KStN 1113 (gp).
PzGrenKp (gp) to KtN 1114 (c) (gp) with two SdKfz 251-equipped platoons.
s Kp (gp) with *Kanonen-Zug, Granatwerfer-Zug, Pionier-Zug*
Supply company

In August 1944, the division was ordered to the Nîmes area in southern France to fight US forces which had landed on the Côte d'Azur during Operation *Dragoon*.

Excerpts from the war diary of PzAufklAbt 11:

6 June 1944: In the early hours of the morning, with the invasion at the English Channel coast begins.
8 June 1944: The bridges over the Dordogne at Le Fleix and St.Foy are blown up by terrorists [French Resistance forces].
15 August 1944: The deployment of the division to the area of Nîmes is dependent on the provision of a crossing over the Rhône. Since all bridges have blown up, the march is delayed.
18 August 1944: Crossing of the Rhône is cancelled.
19 August 1944: At 05:00hrs the division marches to the new crossing area at Arles, Vallabrègues, Aramon and the bridge at Roquemaure north of Avignon. The bridge

Two 8-Rad (Tp) heavy armoured cars in a German town, being prepared for transportation to a front-line combat unit. Note, every second vehicle is fitted with a *Sternantenne* 'd', which indicates they are equipped with a long-range MW transmitter.

is destroyed in an air attack and the crossing is further delayed by traffic jams and continuous air raids.

20 August 1944: New area of operations at Talenge near Coustellet. Forces assigned: 1.Battery with self-propelled 10.5cm, seven PzKpfw IV (*kurz* and *lang*) and a troop of scout cars and a gun platoon as security in the Durance valley.

21 August 1944: Battles with enemy advance units. The enemy loses two Shermans, two armoured scout cars, and an anti-tank gun. Five enemy vehicles were captured, and a truck being used by partisans was destroyed.

22 August 1944: At 17:00hrs, enemy artillery opens a heavy bombardment, which is followed by firefights with US forces. As a result, 4.Kp loses 60 percent of its soft-skinned vehicles. These can be quickly replaced by requisitioned French vehicles.

23 August 1944: Deployment for the attack on Charols and Puy St Martin. A platoon from 2.Kp supported by two PzKpfw IV crossed the bridge at Charols. In response, the enemy opened defensive fire from artillery, anti-tank guns, tanks, mortars, and heavy machine guns. Three armoured carriers and all our tanks were destroyed. Fighting continued with enemy Sherman tanks, and one was knocked-out by an SdKfz 251/9. The battalion was forced to retreat under heavy enemy artillery fire.

All PzAufkl training units were issued all types of armoured reconnaissance vehicles from early to late production batches. Here an early SdKfz 231 and a late SdKfz 232 are used to carry coffins on the occasion of a funeral.

25 August 1944: 2.Kp, as lead company, attacks enemy forces in front of Crest and advances to within 2km of the site. One enemy scout car is captured, a scout car destroyed, six Willys [Jeeps] captured and 14 prisoners taken.

3 September 1944: At 08:30hrs, division orders an attack on Jasseron. This is to be supported by three PzKpfw V *Panther*, four PzKpfw IV (*kurz* or *lang* armed [*]), and 1.*Pionier-Kompanie* (PiKp – engineer company). At 10:00hrs, we contact the enemy in Montrevel. In the village, US forces had entrenched and were blocking the road to the north and a side road to the east. Both 4.Kp and 2.Kp attack and are immediately engaged in heavy house-to-house fighting. We succeed in advancing to the centre of the village. But our tanks cannot follow, since the enemy had hidden a tank by the side of many buildings. One of our PzKpfw IV is knocked out as 4.Kp pushes past enemy positions on the left, while 2.Kp advances metre-by-metre on the right. At 19:00hrs the enemy surrenders.

Success: A total of two US Army reconnaissance squadrons were routed. We captured or destroyed 22 scout cars, three half-track carriers, four trucks, and 19 passenger cars. A total of 145 prisoners were taken and we counted 34 dead. In addition, we liberated 60 German prisoners who had been with the supply company for our division when it was attacked, in the morning hours, at Malafretaz.

Own losses (PzAufklAbt): One 8-Rad and one armoured carrier.

7 September 1944: At 11:00hrs, *Leutnant* Hennrich arrives with four new 8-Rad. At 21.00hrs, 2.Kp has to withdraw, enemy pressure is too strong and it has only five weak groups left. The attached battery of light field artillery has been knocked-out.

Losses (2.Kp): Two dead, and six wounded.

8 September 1944: At 13:00hrs, the enemy broke through positions held by 2.Kp. The enemy launches almost continuous heavy attacks as 2.Kp withdraws and redeployed to the north. The company still has two weak groups.

Losses: One armoured carrier. Gains: two Willys [Jeeps], two motorcycles, six MG. were captured.

On 29 September 1944, the war diary for the period 12 September 1944 to 28 September 1944 was lost some 2.5km west of Bathelémont. It was burned, with many other documents, when the commander's armoured half-track was hit by an Allied fighter-bomber and caught fire. The report continues:

29 September 1944: At 02:15hrs 3.Kp advances to Height 318 and occupies the ground up to the shepherd's hut. Four enemy tanks [Sherman] attack the positions

Only the Ausf B chassis was used for the 7.5cm K51-armed SdKfz 250/8. From mid-1944, each PzAufklKp was issued with two of these vehicles. The SdKfz 250/8 also mounted an MG 42 for self-defence.

held by our flanking company, the fog which had been favouring us disperses around midday, whereupon the enemy begins a heavy artillery bombardment as our company begins to advance. Within a short time, six of our tanks are knocked-out. The enemy is in front of positions held by 4.Kp with three tanks, and another ten enemy tanks are observed behind the hill. At the same time, Allied ground-attack aircraft begin a heavy attack on La Ferme Fourasse.

(*) The high number of PzKpfw IV armed with 7.5cm KwK 37 (*kurz*) L/24 is interesting. After a brief successful counterattack on US units, 11.PzDiv fought northward through the entire Rhône and Saône valleys. In October 1944, after nearly 1,000km, the battle-worn unit reached Lorraine. In December, the division took part in the fighting during the Ardennes offensive.

On 30 January 1945, the *Abteilung Ausbildung* V *(Panzeraufklärer)* (training department [armoured reconnaissance]) submitted to the HWA a report written by *Major* Petri, a front-line officer, to the Inspector General of Tank Troops:

Conclusions drawn after *Unternehmen Wacht am Rhein* [Operation *Vigil* on the Rhine] in the Ardennes [Battle of the Bulge] between 16 December 1944 and 24 January 1945:

The Sdkfz 234/2 *Puma* 7.5cm [*lang*] is good (*). But it is just not clear to me why it was

A column of three late series SdKfz 232 (Fu), from an unknown SS unit, patrol along cobble-paved road alongside a tramway somewhere in Belgium as German forces continued their retreat. The vehicle number was painted directly on the armour without a white border, an unusual detail.

not issued earlier when this issue was first raised. At that time, the request failed due to open questions regarding top-heaviness and the low ammunition supply.

The question of whether to give preference to a 2cm or a 3.7cm weapon has, in my opinion, been completely settled. The ground-attack aircraft is the most dangerous, but since it flies very low it is extremely vulnerable to fire from our 2cm FlaK 38 L/55 cannons. The majority of fighter-bomber kills are made with this weapon. Conversely, medium and heavy bomber aircraft fly at altitudes which are out of range even of our 3.7cm FlaK.

I myself led scouting parties by day with two *Kübelwagens*, a motorcycle and a SdKfz 234/2 *Puma*. With these I tried to fulfill my mission of bringing in fuel and ammunition to trapped units. I was promised a column of 40 trucks, two assault guns and a *Puma* (5cm Fu). Since these were not available in time, I set out at around 16:00hrs, despite it being ideal 'Jabo weather', to find a suitable safe route. After only 3km the Jabos spotted me, despite 'Luki and all chicanery'(**) driving from cover to cover. The ten-minute attack hit my vehicle, shot through fuel tank and punctured three tyres. The armour of the *Puma* was hit several times, but not penetrated. The strafing attack was from the rear, but the *Puma* was a 5cm-armed vehicle, so we were completely defenseless. As far as I am aware, the enemy aircraft have a super-heavy machine gun [20mm

cannon]. I am describing all this in detail, because similar experiences were also brought to my attention by other scout leaders. Our vehicles have a basic advantage, in most cases the armour protects against fire from 0.50-inch machine guns and against bomb splinters. However, the vehicle driver must keep his nerve. Although the enemy dropped 12 bombs on us, none came so close as to even damage our vehicles. (***)

To cut a long story short: The patrol needs a 2cm weapon, but not a 3.7cm. Under the conditions described above, a patrol can be driven even during the day. The *Puma* (2cm) is absolutely capable of defending itself with success.

Furthermore, I noticed that one of our tanks, which had already burned out, was attacked on three consecutive days by enemy fighter-bombers until it received a devastating direct hit. We should work much more often with decoy vehicles to divert some of the low-flying aircraft from real targets.

Statement from the *Generalinspekteur:* The report from Major Petri shows that the 2cm weapon offers the best possibilities for effective combat against enemy low-level air attacks. Particularly in view of this danger, it is imperative that no deviation be made under any circumstances from the present division of the armoured reconnaissance squad into an SdKfz 234/1 (2cm) and an SdKfz 234/4 (7.5cm PaK L/48) in favour of the heavy weapon.

Spring 1945, the last deployment: A very early series SdKfz 221 leads an SdKfz 234/4, followed by an SdKfz 222 past lines of cheering comrades as they leave their barracks, in eastern Germany, for the frontline.

An SdKfz 233 armed with the formidable 7.5cm Kwk L/24 assault gun. The vehicle is in service with PzAufklAbt 4 (4.PzDiv) when it was deployed on the Eastern Front in 1944

(*) This report proves that despite reports to the contrary (including by Thomas Jentz), the 8-Rad (Tp), or SdKfz 234, did receive the distinctive designation *'Puma'*, and apparently this was used for all variants.

(**) 'with Luki and all chicanery', colloquial for advance using the greatest caution.

(***) This view must be taken with great caution. The low-flying attacks were also effective against armoured vehicles. The *Puma* (2cm), unlike the 5cm-armed variant, could effectively engage enemy ground-attack aircraft.

Overall, the report appears confused and taken out of context; it has been reworded for better understanding. However, a clear message is recognizable: for the *Puma*, the 2cm cannon was preferred to the 5cm KwK 39 L/60.

The effectiveness of the 2cm KwK 38 L/55 in repelling enemy low-flying aircraft is also confirmed by a field report from an unknown PzSpKp 'c' in the east, published in the January 1945 issue of the *Nachrichtenblatt der Panzertruppe* (Bulletin of the Armoured Forces).

It is expedient and it has proved valuable to let the PzSpKp 'c' follow the attack by the division and use it for air protection. During a major attack in the spring of 1944, the company managed to shoot down six [Soviet] Ilyushin Il-2 *'Stormovik'* armoured strike aircraft within two days.

Other reports from anti-aircraft units speak a different language. In regard to the heavily armoured ground-attack aircraft (often called *Schlächter* [butcher] by German troops) the effect of the 2cm FlaK 38 L/55 was often described as generally too weak.

In December 1944, the final version of the 8-Rad (Tp) entered front-line service. In an attempt to increase the combat power of the PzAufklAbt, the effective 7.5cm PaK 40 L/48 was installed in the vehicle. By April 1945, some 90 SdKfz 234/4 had been produced and delivered.

In April 1945 a new KStN was issued. The mixed PzSpKp 'f' to KStN 1162 (f) was to have a very high fire power, with nine SdKfz 234/1, eight SdKfz 234/4 and three SdKfz 251/3, in addition to three SdKfz 251/17 (mounting *drilling* MG 151) and three SdKfz 251/22 mounting a 7.5cm PaK 40 L/48.

Both the SdKfz 234/4 and SdKfz 251/22 were referred to as 'PaK-Wagen'. But KStN 1162 (f) was not to be realized until end of the war. All SdKfz 234/4 were to be assigned to the PzAufklAbt as replacements for losses.

Theoretically, the new PzSpKp 'f' would have had a particularly high combat capability, but the unit was created under the impression of a lost war; the defence against enemy tanks was given the utmost priority. The important question of operational combat reconnaissance was pushed into the background.

The SdKfz 222, here a later model armed with a 2cm KwK 38 L/55, was destined to remain in front-line service until the end of the war. Note the tactical sign for 14.PzDiv has been painted next to the exhaust.

Captured Vehicles 10

With the beginning of the war, the limited capacity of German industry began to gradually worsen as the supply of raw materials deteriorated and from 1941 at the latest, the numerical superiority of the enemy's armed forces became clear.

Taken together, this led to various measures:

- Collection and further use of all types of captured material
- Inclusion of armament factories in the occupied nations
- Exploitation of the raw material resources in the above

The German reconnaissance units were affected by this situation, but only to a limited extent.

French Types

The capitulation of France presented the German military with a considerable number of weapons, vehicles and other equipment. These resources were soon recognized and put to the best possible use.

However, in 1940 a new office, the *Zentrale Kraftfahrzeug Versorgungsstelle West* (ZentraKraftWest – central motor vehicle supply agency west), was opened in Paris to organize the recovery and repair of the many damaged or abandoned motor vehicles captured after the invasion. The production facilities of all French industrial companies were also to be evaluated and registered. The task was made even more difficult since the French motor industry was made up of many small manufacturers. Only Renault, Citroën and Peugeot and a few others had factories with facilities for the mass production of vehicles.

Opposite: A column of *Beute* (captured) French-built Panhard P178 armoured cars, in service with 7.PzDiv, advances deep into Russian territory during the first month of *Unternehmen Barbarossa* when German forces attacked on 22 June 1941.

Under the direction of expert German officers, production was successfully restarted. In early 1941, trucks, half-track tractors and passenger cars from French production, as well as repaired British vehicles, were being delivered in large numbers to infantry and armoured divisions. It is certainly no exaggeration to say that the German advance on Moscow in 1941 would not have been possible without these and *Beute* (captured) vehicles.

A letter from Panzer Gruppe 3, dated 10 May, details the problems of this hasty conversion:

> The 20.PzDiv is currently being equipped with French-built commercial vehicles, which have to be delivered from France, and this has been in progress since around 26 April. Training is still very limited. Some 50 percent of our *Kübelwagen* are being replaced by standard production passenger cars (Citroën). These have absolutely no off-road capability and leading from the vehicle is impossible. Instead of personnel carriers, commercial trucks without any off-road capability are being supplied. Half of all motorcycles are being replaced by small passenger cars which with the same level of performance. Apparently, these are also intended for use by the KradSchtzBtl.

Only the Panhard P 178 armoured car was considered to be suitable for use by German reconnaissance troops, development of the type as a long-range reconnaissance vehicle had begun in 1931.

Large numbers of serviceable Panhard P 178 became available to the German military after the fall of France in 1941. This allowed two Panzer divisions (7.PzDiv and 20.PzDiv) to each have a reconnaissance units equipped with the type. In German service the vehicle was designated as the PzSpWg P204(f) – the 'f' indicates *französisch* [French] origin.

The compact bodywork was fabricated from 20mm riveted armour plate and accommodated a crew of four: the commander, a gunner and two drivers: – the reserve (rear) operated the radio. The closed turret housed a 25mm SAT 35 anti-tank gun and a coaxially-mounted 7.5mm Reibel machine gun which gave the P 178 the firepower to successfully fight the poorly armoured PzKpfw I and PzKpfw II at up to a range of 800m. Although it had four-wheel-drive, off-road mobility was severely limited due to poorly designed suspension and only 35cm ground clearance.

In total, some 360 of the type were in service at the start of the war, of which 190 remained operational when France capitulated. During the winter of 1940/41, these vehicles were completely overhauled and designated PzSpWg P204(f) – 'f' indicates *französisch* (French) origin. An unknown number of vehicles had German radio equipment installed; those equipped with FuSprech 'a' transceiver were designated PzSpWg (Fu) P204(f) and those with Fu 12, long-range equipment, were designated PzSpWg (Fu) P204(f). Like the SdKfz 232, heavy armoured reconnaissance vehicles, they were equipped with a frame-type antenna.

Due to their effective armament, these vehicles were absolutely comparable to the German armoured reconnaissance vehicles, which meant that the P 178

This PzSpWg 204(f) was assigned, in 1941, to AufklAbt 20 in the newly formed 20.PzDiv. The almost perpendicular surfaces on the riveted superstructure made the type extremely vulnerable to anti-tank fire.

All PzSpWg P204(f) were fitted with German radio equipment. The vehicle on the left carries a Fu 12 and a frame-type antenna, the other is fitted with a FuSprech 'a' or 'f' and a 2m *Stabantenne*. The divisional sign for 7.PzDiv is visible next to the *Balkenkreuz*.

could be deployed to replace the SdKfz 222 or SdKfz 231/SdKfz 232 in the armoured reconnaissance company according to KStN 1162.

Two reconnaissance battalions, PzAufklAbt 37 attached to 7.PzDiv and PzAufklAbt 92 attached to 20.PzDiv, were fully equipped with these vehicles. The exact numbers are not known, but presumably these battalions each had two PzSpKp, equipped with PzSpWg P204(f).

A status report, dated 8 August 1941, describes the situation within 7.PzDiv. The commander reported two of the three Panzer battalions with 127 vehicles remained operational. The condition of PzAufklAbt 37 is described as satisfactory, but only one of the two PzSpKp remained operational. Some 66 percent of the KradSchtz and 50 percent of the heavy companies were described as combat ready. The general lack of spare parts, especially those for non-German vehicles, certainly led to many avoidable failures.

The commander reported the following shortages:

25 PzSpWg P204(f) (2.5cm *Kanone*)
14 PzSpWg P204(f) (Funk)
Two PzSpWg P204(f) (*Funkstelle* – radio post)
One PzSpWg P204(f) (*Befehlswagen* – command vehicle)

Interestingly, some 43 Panhards were fitted with special wheels to operate on railway track as *Schienenpanzer* (railway defence vehicles) which, from 1942, were deployed to provide security for armoured trains. The type could be quickly converted back to road use.

Under the terms of the German armistice with the Vichy regime, 64 were supplied to police units operating in areas under their control.

Unfortunately, the few reports available provide little detail as to the deployment and performance of the PzSpWg P204(f).

Russian Vehicles

Although the Red Army used wheeled armoured vehicles in relatively small numbers, some were captured during the rapid advance into the Soviet Union. Both the BA-20 and BA-10 were used by German forces and designated PzSpWg 202(r) and PzSpWg 203(r) – 'r' indicates *russisch* (Russian). When a vehicle could be repaired and ready for operations, they were used by German units on a 'when necessary' basis, but the majority of vehicles were delivered *Feldpolizei* (field police) units fighting Russian partisans.

A BA-10 armoured car captured intact from the Red Army by 3.PzDiv in 1941. The vehicle has been painted with conspicuous cross indicating that it was almost immediately used by German forces. Mechanically it was similar to a German PzSpWg (6-Rad), since it also utilized a three-axle chassis from the GAZ-built AAA truck.

Allied Vehicles

From the day the DAK landed in North Africa it suffered from supply problems. Consequently, German troops fighting in the desert were forced to use any vehicle captured intact. A surprising variety of wheeled armoured vehicles were abandoned by British and Commonwealth forces which would be repaired, painted with DAK markings and distributed to German forces to replace shortages.

Italian Vehicles

The Italian armaments and vehicle industries was also to be pressed into German service in a similar way to those in French factories. After Italy capitulated in 1943, their armed forces were disarmed and the existing material was used to replenish German divisions.

One important vehicle was the FIAT-Ansaldo *Autoblindo* (AB – armoured car) 41, some 550 of which were built, which was designed for use on roads or in the arid stony desert regions of colonial Italy. The vehicle was similar to the Panhard P 178 and also had a riveted superstructure. It was fitted with a small rotatable turret mounting a 20mm Breda mod.35 auto-cannon and two 8mm Breda machine guns: one coaxial with the main gun. In 1944, the AB 43 entered service and had a much roomier turret which mounted a 47mm Breda 47/32 M35 anti-tank gun, a significant increase in firepower.

When taken over by German units the Italian type RM 3M radio was

retained, since the frequency range was identical to that of the German 30W. Unlike the French-built Panhard P 178, the vehicles were not automatically integrated into front-line reconnaissance units, but were assigned to various police units operating in the Balkans.

Interestingly, as late as January 1945, the Inspector General of the Panzer Troops suggested setting up a *Panzerspäh-Abteilung* AB 41 using any available serviceable vehicles:

AB 41-equipped PzSpAbt:

The proposed structure of a PzSpAbt AB 41 is presented as an addendum. The PzSpAbt in the proposed structure is for a particularly fast reconnaissance unit that can be rapidly moved on the European road network and benefit from the AB 41 having relatively low fuel consumption. The PzSpAbt, consisting almost exclusively of wheeled vehicles, is expected to be able to cover daily distance of up to 250km without any significant mechanical breakdowns.

The PzSpAbt is designed for wide variety of reconnaissance tasks; its structure prohibits infantry-style combat operations.

The division has 18 armoured reconnaissance squads, of which 12 can be reinforced by assigning 7.5cm (*lang*)-armed SdKfz 234/4. The combination of AB 41 and 8-Rad is not ideal, since the driving characteristics are different and, significantly, both petrol and diesel fuel are needed. However, in order to give the PzSpAbt the armour-piercing weapons it absolutely needs, this composition has to be accepted.

A platoon from PolRgt Bozen on patrol in central Italy. The AB 41 is finished in the distinctive camouflage scheme specifically designed for the region. The type was armed with a coaxially-mounted 20mm Breda mod.35 and an 8mm Breda mod.38 machine gun. The performance of the main gun was equivalent to the German 2cm KwK 35 L/55 tank gun.

Depending on the situation, the PzSpTrp are to be reinforced by assigning a group from the reconnaissance platoon should it require assistance to fulfill a combat mission. A reinforced PzSpTrp should be able to repel enemy reconnaissance mission, fight its way through weak forces and delay the advance of enemy tanks with concentrated fire. But in its current form, the operation of the AB 41 armoured reconnaissance car is badly affected by the distribution of the crew: a principal (front) driver; the commander is also the gunner; a second (rear) driver; and a rear machine gunner/radio operator. Since the turret offers enough space for two men, the vehicle has been modified to a PzSpKp *zur besonderen Vefügung* [zbV – special duties] 468 so that that the commander and gunner

Two PzSpWg 204(f) in service with AufklAbt7 (7.PzDiv) secure a road in a Soviet village during the advance on Moscow. Both vehicles are fitted with the frame-type antenna as used on the SdKfz 232 (8-Rad), which indicates they carry the same radio equipment.

are accommodated in the turret, while the rear driver also assumes the duties of radio operator. This conversion must be carried out on all vehicles assigned to the PzSpKp AB 41, while in the AB 41 (*Funkstelle*) assigned to the *Nachrichten-Zug* [intelligence platoon] it is more sensible to retain the original distribution of the crew.

The PzSpWg AB 41 has a closed turret and consequently is not suitable for anti-aircraft defence. Additionally, the battalion has almost no anti-aircraft weapons, which must be taken into account when it is deployed in the western or south-western theatre of war. (The lack of anti-aircraft weapons is acceptable for a PzSpAbt, since it is divided into various reconnaissance units according to task and structure.)

This organizational structure for a PzAufklAbt was produced in 1945. It shows that military planners proposed for it to be equipped with a large number of AB 41 armoured cars captured from the Italian army. Note, the artillery platoon was to be issued with 7.5cm StuK L/24-armed SdKfz 234/4.

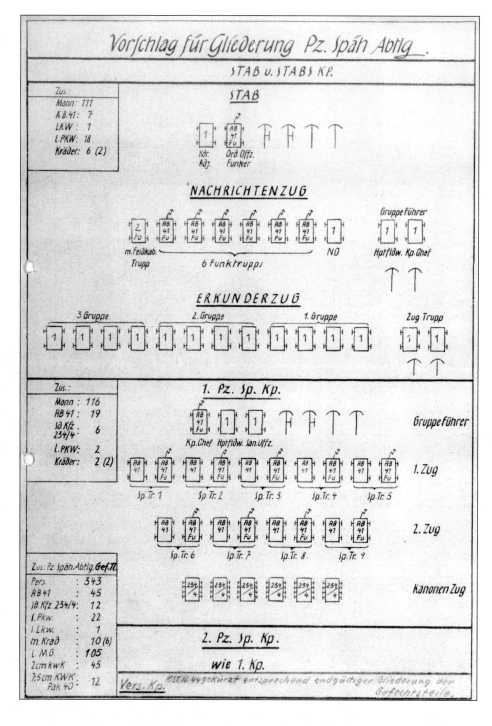

In addition to the Italian RM 3M radio, FuSprech 'f' transceiver had to be installed to ensure communication with platoons equipped with the SdKfz 234/4.

It seems probable that this arrangement was created in order to form as many reconnaissance elements as possible in the final months of the war by utilizing all serviceable AB 41. It is not known to what extent it was planned to continue or expand AB 41 production of the type. This, too, is an indication of the generally desolate supply situation of the German army.

Nevertheless, it seems unlikely that this structure was implemented on a larger scale.

Interestingly German military planners never considered captured armoured cars to be of any importance for the reconnaissance troops.

Final Assessment

With the build-up of the new *Wehrmacht*, and the PzTrp, considerable financial resources were also expended to create modern reconnaissance units.

Engineers from an unknown SS unit have replaced the Russian 7.62m Degtyarev (DT) machine gun armament with an MG34. Some of these lightly armoured vehicles, carried a frame antenna and it is probable that German intelligence used the Soviet-built radio to intercept signals between enemy units on the battlefront.

A FIAT-Ansaldo AB 41, from PolRgt Bozen, leaves a Siebel *Fähre* (ferry) which were used for crossing the many wide rivers and lakes in eastern Europe. The vessel could be armed with up to four 8.8cm FlaK guns, 2cm *Flakvierling* 38 L/55 in a quadruple mounting, and two 2cm FlaK 30 L/55 for anti-aircraft defence.

As in the case of the Panzer divisions, forward-looking decisions were taken that gave the Germans a distinct advantage over their opponents in the early campaigns. The task of tactical, and within certain limits operational, reconnaissance could be successfully fulfilled with the means available.

While the armament of the AufklAbt proved to be sufficient at the beginning of the war, a dangerous gap became evident when engaging an armoured force.

When the reconnaissance battalions were merged with the KradSchtz battalions in 1942, new effective units were created that had significantly increased combat effectiveness. The firepower of these units was also increased by the introduction of the 7.5cm KwK L/24 on the SdKfz 233 (8-Rad) and also the SdKfz 250/8 and SdKfz 251/9 half-tracks, to provide effective supporting fire.

This considerably expanded the range of tasks for the reconnaissance units, but this was not without problems, since they were often deployed to reinforce battle groups and had to neglect their regular duties.

At first the *Rad-Panzerspähwagen* (wheeled armoured cars) proved to

be of significant value on the battlefront, but when the war expanded with the invasion of the Soviet Union the weather conditions soon revealed their limitations. In 1942, the introduction of half-tracked carriers only partially compensated for the lack of off-road mobility.

Although considered essential, the conversion of the PzAufklAbt to fully-tracked vehicles was never completely achieved and only a few units received semi-developed solutions. While the PzKpfw V *Panther* was successfully introduced in 1943, the development of a modern light reconnaissance tank that could also be deployed for reconnaissance never materialized.

As the end of the war drew closer, a number of significant vehicles were delivered to the battlefront and included the SdKfz 234/4, mounting 7.5cm PaK 40 heavy anti-tank gun, and also the SdKfz 251/22 which carried the same weapon on a hopelessly overloaded chassis. Behind this was an ultimately desperate but totally futile attempt to equip reconnaissance units with an effective anti-tank defence.

By 1945, the men of the reconnaissance troop were mostly involved in fighting a defensive battle on the frontlines around Berlin.

This AB 41, from an unknown unit, has been abandoned during the final battle for Berlin, the capital of the Reich. Note the rear-mounted 8mm Breda mod.38 machine gun.

Index

Two PzKpfw II Ausf L *'Luchs'* from PzAufklAbt 4 (4.PzDiv): Crewmen from the leading tank wind up the *Schwungkraftanlasser* (inertia starter) in order to save the vehicle's batteries.

1941: Elements of a PzAufklAbt prepare to cross a bridge over the Miljacka river, near the city of Sarajevo, as German forces continued their advance into the Balkans. The column is led by an SdKfz 221 while a SdKfz 232, armed with a 2cm KwK 30 L/55, stands guard.

Acknowledgements

The author evaluated a vast amount of information that was searched for and found in a number of public archives including, Bundesarchiv/Militärarchiv (BAMA), Freiburg, Germany; the National Archives & Records Administration (NARA), Washington, USA and also the internet-based project for digitizing German documents in archives of the Russian Federation.

All documentation found was evaluated thoroughly in the context of their historical background and represent a significant portion of the book.

The technical side of reconnaissance was extensively evaluated in the *Panzer Tracts* series produced by the late Thomas Jentz and Hilary L. Doyle, which I recommend for further information. I also used books written by Walter J. Spielberger as a source and inspiration. Other post-war publications were used only to a limited extent.

The many long conversations with late *Oberst* Berndt von Mitzlaff – he was involved with the expansion of the German reconnaissance force from the beginning – were very important to the author.

Peter Müller (Historyfacts) kindly provided much valuable information. To my editor Jasper Spencer-Smith, that ever-patient gentleman, for his guidance and work on my manuscript. Also, thanks to Crispin Goodall who took over the design and layout at very short notice.

The following people granted me access to their collections: Florian von Aufseß, Jürgen Wilhelm, Wolfgang Schneider, Karlheinz Münch, Henry Hoppe, Markus Zöllner and Holger Erdmann.

All images in this book are, unless otherwise credited, from the Thomas Anderson Collection.

Bibliography

Doyle. H & Jentz. T: *Panzer Tracts*, various editions – Panzer Tracts, Boyds, ML, USA
Jentz. T: *Die Deutschen Panzertruppen*, Volumes 1 & 2 – Podzun-Pallas Verlag, Eggolsheim, Germany.
Tessin. G: *Verbände und Truppen der Deutschen Wehrmacht* – E.S. Mittler & Sohn, Hamburg, Germany.